SUN-SIGN REVELATIONS

SUN-SIGN REVELATIONS

A Practical, Unflattering,
Lighthearted Guide to the Personalities
of our Friends and Ourselves

Maria Elise Crummere

THE BODLEY HEAD
LONDON SYDNEY
TORONTO

FOR DOLORES BONSEIGNEUR

Copyright © by Maria Elise Crummere 1974
ISBN 0 370 10361 0
Printed and bound in Great Britain for
The Bodley Head Ltd
9 Bow Street, London W C 2 7 A L
by Redwood Burn Limited, Trowbridge & Esher
First published in Great Britain 1974

CONTENTS

INTRODUCTION

I F YOU BUY a book on astrology to learn about your character or personality, about the quality of your reasoning or your ability to make the correct selection of a profession, marriage partner, or path through life, you naturally turn to the chapter that gives a general description of your sign. Writers of astrological books and popular magazine or newspaper columnists want to please you, so they tell you about all the virtues and admirable traits of your sign. If they didn't, you would be disappointed.

For example, they will say that Aries is the self-appointed hero, the front-runner who gets credit for being a pioneer, the brave and courageous leader. They will tell you that Taurus is the reliable money-maker, that he belongs in some responsible financial position because he can assess the economic situation with accuracy. Gemini will be pleased to find that his sign is generally that of a writer, speaker, teacher, theatrical director, or leader in the art world. Cancer is described as the representative of the public who knows the needs of the people and has both the desire and the ability to meet them. And Leo is the dramatic lover, who either portrays love in the theater or acts it out in life, as the beneficent ruler or as Lady Bountiful. Virgo, the servant par excellence, supervises the world with supreme executive ability and keeps everything in working order. Libra, the beauty-conscious sign, tends to be charming, lovely, well-dressed, surrounded by elegance—not an ugly sound or a distressing note is to be heard, for to achieve the peace and calm Librans crave, all unpleasantness must be avoided. Then there is Scorpio, who has an indomitable force in his nature that drives him to carry all endeavors to perfection. A Sagittarian expects the books to emphasize his brilliant mind; he is the traveler who knows the world, the bon vivant, the lawyer or scholar who is knowledgeable about world affairs. Capricorn is not surprised to note that his character is one of integrity, breeding—the sort who becomes president of a large corporation. Aquarius will find that he belongs in the Hall of Fame. He is the humanitarian of the zodiac, cool, detached, yet the great friend of mankind. Pisces is generally noted for his compassion, for the sacrifices he makes. He is willing to share the misfortunes of others. These are a few of the many virtues the reader expects and desires to believe about himself.

After you have read yet another virtuous description of yourself, what is the outcome? Do these standard analyses of the sun signs follow through by telling you of all the variables that appear in everyone's astrological chart? Do their predictions mean anything? How frustrating to be told of your good points and never hear a word about why you might not succeed or excel in your chosen field. How can you be expected to make all the right moves that your so-called virtues guarantee without knowing what your weak points might be?

First of all, you may have only one planet* in your birth sign—your Sun—and the other nine planets (i.e., the Moon and all of the planets *except* the Earth) may be distributed in quite disparate signs. For example, your mentality depends on the position of the Moon at the moment of your birth, while your love nature is ruled by the position of Venus and the manner in which your energies function depends upon the position of Mars. The planet governing your future is Saturn, and your ability to respond to change is ruled by Uranus. Your envisioned goals are governed by Neptune, while your opinions and judgments are controlled by Jupiter. Mercury is the planet of practical reasoning, while Pluto, the latest planet to be discovered, rules the world of politics and ideologies. The history-makers are the big five: Jupiter, Saturn, Uranus, Neptune, and Pluto. They stand high above the other five, the daily workers, through their respective powers of judgment, plan, change, progress, and beliefs. Each of these planets will be present in every chart in a different position and relationship (or aspect) to each other, and these infinite variations from chart to chart explain the infinite variations in individuals, even those born under the same sun sign. Another important influence on a person's chart is the rising sign, or ascendant, which is the zodiacal sign that was passing over the eastern horizon at the moment of your birth. It is this sign that will modify the basic physical appearance and approach to life as determined by your sun sign. Only if you were born near sunrise would your sun sign and ascendant be the same, and only in that case would the general description offered by newspapers and magazines come close to the real you.

Even taking all these complicated factors into account,

* The word *planet* in astrology does not have the same scientific meaning as it does in astronomy. Although the sun and moon are not really planets, they are classified that way in astrology.

however, why doesn't your present existence bear out the glamorous description you are promised by most astrologers? Why does the wonderful future guaranteed you so often fail to materialize? It is very simple. The popular astrologers are afraid of you, their public. They know what you want and expect to hear, and they know that if they fail to reassure you of an exciting destiny, you will not buy their pamphlets, attend their lectures, or solicit their services. If the predictions they give you fail, they will suggest that you have not followed their advice, which indeed you may not have done. They will say that you did not properly time the event that would have led to fortune, or that you did not deal amicably with others to gain your advantage, or that you did not act on a well-aspected Jupiter, or whatever. All of this could be true. Nevertheless, the astrologer has undoubtedly left out some of the most important facts evident on the chart. He or she knows that you will only accept the good or positive aspects of your character. It is about time that we looked at what you really are instead of at what the conventional astrological texts say you are. Following the general descriptions of each sign in this book is a separate section that briefly tells the influence the rising sign will have on the sun sign. Needless to say, I do not expect to find in yourself or in others all of the negative characteristics any more than I would expect you to believe all the positive descriptions you find elsewhere. But you may find this a refreshing and useful guide, and you won't be unnecessarily surprised or hurt by certain kinds of behavior in your friends or associates—or in yourself.

ARIES

The Egomaniac

March 21 to April 19

T HERE are many ancient metaphysical subjects that reveal mysteries of man's existence but the one that has no peer, in terms of both spiritual and practical application, is astrology, since it contains the design of man's progress through life. No other subject can time an event in one's life so that what one wills can take place. Man's will is ruled by the position of the sun at the time of birth, and the sun represents the will for survival, power, and accomplishment.

Those born under the sign of Aries, the first sign of the zodiac to spring into life as the sun crosses into the first quarter of the spring equinox, are the starters, the initiators. Aries is the first cardinal sign and the first fire sign—cardinal for action, fire for excitement. The symbol for Aries is made up of two half moons joined by a straight line, which indicates authority. The symbol resembles the horns of the ram, the animal symbol of the sign, as well as the eyebrows and nose of man, the part of the body ruled by Aries. The symbol for Mars, the planet that rules Aries, is made up of a circle and a variation of the cross; the cross at the top represents matter (or practicality) and the circle is the sun, the source of energy.

Those born under the sign of Aries possess these qualities in one degree or another, but their outstanding characteristic is an enormous ego, an exaggerated concentration on the self, hence "the egomaniac."

Physical Appearance
Aries tends to red or gold coloring, and the complexion is usually ruddy. The large cranium is wide from temple to temple; the planes of the face are flat, and the nose clings to the cheek line somewhat defensively. The mouth is wide, though the lips lack an outward curve, and the teeth are large. The Aries smile is easy and generous, and the eyes are humorous. The body moves quickly and eagerly, and is muscular and lean. The Aries approach is open and forthright, full of self-assurance though often impatient. Quickness of impulse is the easiest way to identify Aries.

Personality
Aries is an active sign, the initiator of all action on the

zodiac, and those born under Aries are extroverts and adventurers. They do not wait for things or people to come to them but go out to get what they want for themselves. Arians are always in a hurry and become very impatient with slow movers and bored with anything that takes too much time to accomplish. They are constantly in search of new adventures, new ideas, new relationships. The beginning of any new program or friendship is what they love most. Because Aries is a fire sign, Arians can stimulate excitement in others and they are good organizers. But they must be allowed to run the show, because if they are thwarted in any way, trouble occurs. They may start a fight or simply try to humiliate those who interfere with them. At first their attack will seem humorous or good-natured, but as the situation becomes more serious, contempt will surface and Aries' egomaniacal traits will begin to show. Arians believe that no one can do anything as well as they can. They are never halfhearted in their criticism of others but cold and derisive; if angry, they mean to hurt their opponents and browbeat them into submission.

Arians are contentious and love to fight. In an argument they will settle for nothing short of surrender, though they will dismiss anyone who will readily relinquish a difference in view—this is a sign of cowardice, the trait Arians despise most. If Aries should fail, he will simply withdraw until the pain of failure has diminished. It is very dangerous to lord it over a failed Aries, for he will strike back without mercy. Arians never analyze the reasons for their failures because they are convinced that others are responsible. The exaggerated Aries ego cannot accept the fact that he has lost, for winning is everything.

When Aries first becomes involved in a new idea, he will give all of his energy and attention to it. One must get everything out of him at the start, when he is still full of enthusiasm. If you are trying to enlist Aries in a new project, do not tell him everything about it at the beginning; tell him a little at a time to keep his interest and excitement fresh. He cannot maintain his enthusiasm over a period of time. As soon as he begins to be bored, his interest wanes and his activity slows down very quickly, until he has nothing more to give. If he hits a snag, if someone is not as enthusiastic as he is, if he feels threatened, he will feel unappreciated and lose complete interest in a project. You must continue to flatter him

and boost the Arian ego so that the first burst of enthusiasm will not subside.

Aries is a pioneer, a ground breaker, but if the tractor
should stop in the middle of the first row in the field, Aries
may never return to finish the job he has begun.

Aries is the one fire sign incapable of bringing anything to a conclusion; he has no staying power but runs
from one thing to another, requiring continual refueling
and reinforcement. As the first fire sign, Aries has even
less perseverance than the others; he is a fast-blazing
bonfire by comparison with the steady burning flame of
Leo or the inconstant flickering fire of Sagittarius. Only
by moving to a new source of interest can his energy be
revived.

Aries is a fine game player so long as the game is a
short one. He is competitive and loves to win but when
the time runs out the game is finished, and he is completely worn out, and glad to move on to a new game, to
start all over again.

Love
When the male Aries falls in love, he feels a tremendous
burst of power. His love is at its peak when the affair is
new; his depth of feeling and his warmth begin to diminish the further the affair progresses. At the beginning of
a love affair Aries can be the ideal lover, but when it ends
there is resentment and even hate. Mars, the ruling planet,
is capable of intense bitterness in adversity. Aries wel-
comes love readily but cannot endure any tests of his love
or demands from the loved one. As in all emotional situations, Aries must be the master; the game must be played
according to his rules. Mars is the warrior who wins
through domination rather than by making any appeal
for approval or affection. Aries can handle more than one
love affair at a time and doesn't worry about hurting his
lover.

The female Aries will woo her loved one rather than be
wooed, and if her lover tries to take the upper hand, she
will dismiss him as difficult and overbearing. She will go
from one man to another, comparing and testing them to
decide which one she can handle with the greatest ease.
Her satisfaction depends entirely on how much the man
is capable of giving her; she rarely if ever considers her
own contribution to the affair. Faithfulness is not a con-
cept she can understand.

Since all fire signs are dramatic and romantic, Aries

will expect these qualities in any love affair. Aries egotism demands complete submission and constant excitement. Since Aries is a male sign, the men are naturally more attractive. The arrogance of the female Aries makes her offensive to most sensitive men, and she is often devoid of femininity.

Marriage

The male Aries settles happily into marriage at first, for it gives him an opportunity to establish a setting in which he is the master—a showplace where he can invite his friends to give their approval of his accomplishments, his social position. His wife is expected to make a good showing, to supply his needs, and to see that he gets the attention he feels he deserves. After the honeymoon, however, Aries will begin to look elsewhere for stimulation and new excitement. There is a continual coming and going in an Aries marriage; the husband will often be away on business trips, but this can help preserve the marriage in the long run. If the wife does not interfere with her husband's longing to go away, and if she greets his return with pleasure and praise, his interest in her will be refreshed and the marriage will be revived. The Aries husband takes his frequent trips in order to retreat and to reassess in peace the strength of his mate's love. The Aries female will also leave her husband from time to time, on trips or love affairs, to reinforce his love of her, to reassure herself that she is wanted. Constant activity gives Aries a kind of power and the knowledge that marriage has not stifled his energy.

Aries does not consider himself bound to his mate. He is greedy and always wants more of something—perhaps recognition or the feeling that he is still attractive to others. His mate must constantly sing his praises, and if his mate fails to feed his ego, Aries will move on to a new partner without hesitation.

Parenthood

The Aries father is proud of his children and wants to ensure them a place in history. John D. Rockefeller, who had Aries rising, made sure that his descendants would carry on in the path he had laid out for them. Aries treats his children as equals, with no coddling or baby talk. Oversensitive children pose a problem for him because he does not understand them. The Aries father loves his offspring and is truly generous to them, but he ex-

pects a good show in return. No parent suffers more than
Aries if the child does not measure up to his expectations.
He demands their admiration and can be quite childish
himself if they do not treat him with the proper respect.
He will become brusque and will refrain from tenderness
in order to inspire the child to develop strength and
courage.

The Aries mother, although as generous as the father,
will never grant them the same importance. She always
wants to keep the upper hand and may even intimidate
them by her relentless pursuit of her own interests outside
the home. She wants the best for her children but she
will not sacrifice her own goals to care for them. The
children of an Aries mother must become accustomed to
her frequent absence. She will show a general interest in
her children but it is neither deep nor long-lasting; she
will give them what she has but not what she is.

Friendship
Because Aries will become violently jealous of another's
ability or accomplishment friendships tend to be insecure
and short-lived. He loves to be surrounded by admirers
and will give many parties in order to be in the center of
the stage, to command a private audience for his many
stories, of which he is always the hero. He loves telling
others how he has managed to accomplish the impossible;
his favorite tales usually involve situations in which he
has rescued a friend or outwitted an enemy. If a guest
should tell a story of his own, Aries will quickly follow up
with a better one in order to reclaim the spotlight. If, in
a conversation, Aries is uninformed on a subject in which
his companion is well-versed, he will become insulting
and try to distract attention back to himself—often in a
vicious way.

An Aries I know gives dinner parties for friends in
different professions when he needs their favors or advice.
He will begin by praising each guest enthusiastically to
keep them from becoming aware that they are being
used. As soon as he has acquired the information he needs,
the party is over. If a guest fails to respond, Aries manages to humiliate him in such a way that he feels unworthy of the hospitality that has been lavished upon him.
Because Aries truly believes in his own superiority, he
can be harsh and merciless when his ego is attacked.
Watching others suffer under his rather sadistic treat-

ment gives him a kind of pleasure that reinforces his egotistical behavior.

The female Aries can be a virago whose arrogance enables her to ride roughshod over both men and women. Men of less aggressive signs are forced to run from her in order to preserve their masculinity. Aries women often find themselves alone and unloved as they reach the end of their lives. Strong men will not submit to these demeaning relationships, and weak men will do their best to escape. The Aries woman will do anything to overcome the threat of a rival and to bring the limelight back to herself. She will not allow the conversation to center on another person. One Aries woman enthusiastically began a friendship with a professional woman by pretending that she had important connections that could help promote the other's efforts. As time went on and the friend pressed for help, the Aries woman would either leave town or become ill until, after months of promises, it became clear that the whole thing was a hoax. The Aries woman seemed to derive great pleasure from the embarrassment she had wrought. By causing frustration in a person who was in a position she envied, she was able to assure herself of her own power and influence.

Career

Because Aries is an energetic sign that can inspire activity in others, Arians make good foremen, leaders, or directors, as long as they are given positions of authority. But they must command others or they will lose interest in whatever they are doing. As in every other aspect of their lives, Arians are best at the beginning of a project, but because they cannot maintain enthusiasm, they leave the completion of the job up to others.

As an athlete and a game player, Aries will often be found playing baseball, football, or tennis. This love of physical display will often extend itself to the theater, politics, or the military—professions ideally suited to Aries' love of power and his relentless pursuit of success. Dwight D. Eisenhower, for example, had Aries rising.

Whatever career Aries chooses, however, the rewards must be great, particularly in terms of public recognition. As he grows older, he becomes increasingly concerned with the way in which he will be remembered in history. He wants to be sure that he will always be thought of as an important figure, and that others will continue to share his own image of himself.

Aries born near sunrise will have Aries rising, and the description given will be exact.

The Taurus ascendant will make Aries very strongly built and dark, with pleasanter, more feminine features.

Gemini rising will give Aries the ability to talk well and will reduce his egomania, making this the most attractive Aries of all.

The Cancer ascendant will add gentleness and shyness to Aries. He will be less aggressive and robust in his behavior.

The Leo ascendant will give Aries a sunny personality and a shorter body.

Virgo rising will make Aries very hard-working; he may criticize others but he will be neat and will stick to his job.

Libra, the sign opposite Aries, will contribute a beautiful, well-formed, and well-coordinated body.

When Scorpio rises for Aries, the personality will be very powerful; a strong combination.

Sagittarius will make Aries tall, less aggressive, and less egotistical.

The Capricorn ascendant will give Aries a more conservative personality, a small physical build, and a more serious demeanor.

If Aquarius is the ascendant, Aries will be tall, which is unusual, and very exciting.

When Pisces rises, Aries' overbearing manner will disappear; he will use a soft approach as a subtle means to monopolize the situation and to attract attention.

TAURUS

The Insensitive Bully

April 20 to May 20

T AURUS is the second sign of the zodiac. It is the first fixed sign and the first earth sign—fixed for determination, earth for practicality. The symbol for Taurus resembles the chin and Adam's apple in the human throat. This symbol represents the horns of the bull, which point upward, forming a cup. During the Golden Age of antiquity, the bull was the symbol of material power, the golden calf an idol representing wealth rather than spirituality. The planet ruling Taurus is Venus, which rules love and harmony, whose symbol is a combination of the circle of the sun and the cross of matter. The cross is below the sun, indicating that the energy is forced down toward the earth, toward physicality, rather than upward toward spiritual power.

Taurus

Venus

Taurus is not a thinker but the sign is practical, often greedy. The outstanding characteristic is a thick skin which makes Taurus insensitive to the rights of others, unresponsive and overbearing, a bully.

Physical Appearance
The shape of the Taurian head is round and compact; the shoulders are high and square, and the neck is very short. The complexion is clear and often beautiful, and the eyes are large, round, and often staring. The nose can be either small, retroussé, and well-formed, or large with a bulb at the tip. The curved lips pout slightly and the teeth are small and even. Taurus has the strongest chin of the zodiac; it is always wide and purposeful, and it sometimes juts forward in a determined bulldog fashion.

The body is sturdy with a thick chest, which is sometimes barrel-shaped. The torso is heavy, the buttocks are flat, and the thighs and legs are thick and muscular. Taurus's feet are always large and fleshy, and the carriage is cumbersome, steady, and plodding.

Personality
Taurus has a quiet, affectionate manner, which seems to indicate a distinctly low-keyed charm. The voice is soft and low, with an occasional bell-like tone, and the speech is unpretentious, often downright simple and rural in inflection. The steady gaze gives an overall impression of innocence, which is misleading, for no sign is so astute in

13

evaluating its environment; Taurians can quickly determine the weight, size, and measure of everything and everyone they see. Life speaks to Taurus in terms of money or value, and until one's status or worth has been gauged and one's potential estimated, the cautious quiet manner will be maintained.

Taurians are basically introverted and depend entirely on instinct to guide them in any relationship; feeling rather than intellect is what moves them. They are defensive and suspicious in the face of the unknown. They are always prepared to accuse others of trying to take advantage of them, for this is the way they themselves behave. One must not appear inquisitive with Taurians if one wants to gain their trust. They can be shrewd but they are not bright or farseeing, and they are the great blunderers of the zodiac.

Taurians are self-indulgent, particularly in a physical way, and they constantly try to appease their strong appetites—they love food, drink, and comfortable surroundings. Although they do not dress fashionably (unless Gemini is present on the chart), they like physical adornment and clothes that will give them status and respectability, the look they cultivate most carefully.

Taurians have little pride but a great deal of inner vanity, which insulates them from ridicule and humiliation. Like all earth signs, Taurians know that they arouse prejudice in others, and their main defense is a hostile attitude, often masked by their silent manner. They do not talk very much so that they can hide their mental weaknesses; they have bad memories and cannot remember what you have said. They are patient in a bovine way, being extremely stubborn and slow to move, though their jealousies and angers are as powerful and deep-seated as they are hidden. Hitler, whose sun was in Taurus, never drank or smoked, took a bland diet, and maintained an attitude of respectability for years before showing his destructive, hysterical rage to the world.

Taurians have no imagination. It takes them a long time to absorb and comprehend a new idea because they have the slowest minds of the zodiac. It is difficult to get and keep their attention in conversation, and they do not listen if the conversation does not concern them or profit them in any way. But they will attach themselves like leeches to anyone who appears to be wealthy or influential, for this is how they gain strength and control over others.

In love the male Taurus will always choose someone inferior to himself, someone whose health is not strong or who is willing to serve him in some way—a kind of servant to wait on him, to be useful in helping him advance his career. Many Taurians choose not to fall in love, for they need their freedom in order to pursue their business interests. For them, love is an unnecessary distraction that might interfere with their career. Taurians are practical in love above all else. This is particularly true for the Taurus woman, who has only marriage in mind.

Taurians hate to talk about love, most of all when a verbal commitment is expected of them. They can never avow their love with a full heart, always fearing that they will be victimized. Freud, a Taurian, was engaged for many years before taking the final step. Taurus cannot bring himself to tell his loved one how much he cares. He is a clumsy lover, knowing he cannot be tender. Taurus will deliberately avoid a delicate emotional situation lest his awkwardness and his inability to deal with it become apparent.

Marriage

Taurians fall in love with a potentially suitable marriage partner at first sight. They will do everything to maintain a steady relationship, though it can be destroyed if the partner tries to become an equal. They cannot abide rivalry, especially when their mate is involved. The home is very important to Taurus as a showplace where he can display the possessions that reflect his power and strength. He also enjoys a garden, where he can show off the results of his green thumb. Frequent guests are welcome because their acceptance of Taurus's hospitality reinforces his feeling of control over others. Yet he is cheap. One Taurus who has a beautiful house herds his friends into a miserable little sunporch after showing off the rest of the house, which remains unused.

As soon as a successful Taurus husband has achieved the kind of household he wants—one that intimidates visitors with its grandeur—he will treat his mate with smug indifference and even cruel abuse until her services are required again to satisfy his often excessive, self-indulgent needs.

If a male Taurian's marriage fails, a servant can easily take over the role of housekeeper, though the man will desire companionship. Otherwise he can become a weighty bore, interested only in his own affairs and unable to communicate with others.

The Taurian woman is like a siren who will charmingly and quietly beguile and seduce a man into marriage and then proceed to strip him bare of all his worldly goods, abandoning him the moment his pockets are empty. She will use her earthy sexual powers, which can be considerable, thanks to the ruling planet Venus, to make a good marriage, repeating the process as often as necessary to satisfy her greed.

Parenthood

Taurus parents want their children to do well, and they carefully choose the kind of education that will enable the child to support himself well—perhaps to carry on the father's business. They are not demonstrative in their affection, fearing they may lose authority or control. The Taurian father is usually respected by his child but he is not understood—which suits Taurus very well. The Taurian parent will supply his child with all the physical comforts but he demands that the youngster wait on him and often overburdens him with chores.

The Taurian mother is somewhat more lenient because she expects favors from her child, perhaps even support later in life. She does not, however, spend much time with her child, preferring to be out shopping (Taurians are shrewd shoppers, sometimes even shoplifters). She will feed and care for her children in order to make them comfortable, but she loves comfort herself; indeed, she can sit all day, indulging herself and selfishly watching her offspring do chores for her. She does not take much interest in her child's education, for she is not a reader or an intellectual in any way, but she will brag about any child who becomes successful and hope that his success will be taken as a sign of her own status and respectability.

Friendship

Because any friends of Taurus are expected to help him gain success in the world, they are always cultivated with care. Taurus will be quick to estimate the potential usefulness of a person and will begin a steady campaign to enlist that friend's trust and support—particularly in terms of making new contacts with others who can further Taurus's goals. If the friend fails to prove useful he is quietly dropped, and Taurus will look elsewhere. A Taurus woman will make herself the confidante to a more powerful, wealthier woman in the hope of an eventual return, while a Taurus man is capable of waiting patiently for the demise or retirement of older associates who might make him their successor.

Taurians always hope to elicit expensive gifts from their friends, yet they themselves give paltry, inexpensive, practical presents. They make a business of describing to guests in an enthusiastic manner the gifts that other guests have brought, hoping the embarrassment will generate some generosity. Taurians are always disappointed when guests arrived empty-handed. They also worry about who will pick up the check when they are dining out with friends.

Taurians make the least significant contribution to a social situation, yet they expect the greatest results. They feel that everyone else present is responsible for making the occasion a success while they sit back and greedily take in food, drink, praise, flattery. All the while they are counting up how much they have gained, how little it cost, and how far ahead of the game they are in terms of friendship. If the total is unsatisfactory, those responsible are dropped from the list of friends. Taurians harbor resentments and never forget a slight, particularly if it has touched their vanity.

Taurus does not always use or exploit his friends; often he will simply require companionship or someone to serve him. In this case he will choose a social inferior. Because Taurus loves to be flattered he is often an easy mark for panhandlers or parasites. He will attract odd individuals, often of a bad sort, because being amoral himself he cannot distinguish between good and bad in others. This does not bother him, as long as his needs are filled.

Career

Taurus does not like hard work, but he has a great respect for money and material wealth and will work steadily toward achieving whatever it is he values. He is a shrewd shopper, a born comparison buyer, and loves to find a bargain—or, best of all, something for nothing. On the other hand, he always expects to receive the highest price for anything he is selling. However, Taurus rarely sells for he likes to accumulate possessions, money, and land. Many Taurians are bankers.

Taurus has a green thumb. Since he prefers the slower-paced country to the city, he is often a farmer. He will wait patiently for results, for his investment to grow in value, for his fields to ripen and show a profit. Taurus works quietly, often in secret, so that it is always a surprise to find that his enterprises have turned out successfully. He can be irritable and nervous while waiting for something to hatch, because his determination to see a plan through to completion is obsessive and he cannot bear interference.

Because Taurians strive for security and solidity, they have great respect for institutions—governmental, financial, and religious. Taurians work well within an institutional setup, not only because it gives them respectability but also because they enjoy working quietly under superiors, from whom they gain personal strength, and above inferiors, whom they can exploit to their own ends and push around in an impersonal, high-handed way.

Taurus born near sunrise will have Taurus rising, and the description given will be exact.

Gemini rising produces a gayer, more versatile Taurus who enjoys being involved in everything.

Cancer rising will make Taurus home loving, generous, and easy to get along with.

Leo will make Taurus generous—less involved with making money, more involved with making friends.

The Virgo ascendant can produce a successful if not very exciting Taurus.

Libra rising makes Taurus a double Venus, so he will be beautiful but pleasure seeking and self-loving.

Scorpio will give Taurus an intense and exclusive personality whose main goal will be power rather than money.

Sagittarius rising will make Taurus less money-grubbing, more enjoyable, and less demanding.

Capricorn ascendant will make Taurus even more dutiful and responsible—a heavy combination.

Aquarius rising will give Taurus a friendly but cool personality, detached yet interesting.

Pisces rising will make Taurus's personality easier to bear, more sympathetic, and very pleasant.

The Aries ascendant will make Taurus exciting and active and will give him a sense of adventure.

GEMINI

The Divine Discontent

May 21 to June 21

G EMINI is the third sign of the zodiac. It is the first
mutable sign and the first air sign—mutable for
duality, air for intelligence. It is the first human sign of
the twelve. Aries is the ram, Taurus is the bull, but
Gemini is the twins. The dual symbol for Gemini is two
straight lines, representing the human lungs or arms,
which Gemini controls, and resembling the two pillars of
wisdom, such as those seen on temples of learning.
Mercury, the ruler of Gemini, is the planet of mind and
reason. The symbol of Mercury is made up of the circle
of the sun or energy, supported by the cross of matter (or
practicality), and topped by the cup of the moon of consciousness, which represents Gemini's eternal striving
upward toward intellectual satisfaction.

Gemini

Mercury

Gemini's constant drive to higher objectives, coupled with
a dual nature that sees both sides to every question and
is therefore indecisive, invariably results in dissatisfaction
and frustration—a continual state of discontentment.

Physical Appearance
Geminis are perennial teen-agers in appearance, always
looking younger than they really are. The head is round,
though not as compact as Taurus. The beautiful, flowing
hair curls in a childlike way at the temples, and the alert
eyes are always full of humor and inspire confidence. The
nose is small and upturned; the lips are well-formed, curv-
ing outward. The complexion is clear, sometimes freckled.
The friendly, eager smile, in which the lips clear the gum
line, exposes teeth that are very small and even. The
neck is long, even swanlike in the most beautiful Geminis, and the body is slight. The arms are long and the
hips remain straight and youthfully slim throughout life.
The thighs and legs are symmetrical and move with great
agility; the hands and feet are small and delicate. The
Gemini gait is light, easy, and rapid; the carriage is
straight and controlled.

Personality
Geminis are practical thinkers and do not like to waste
time unless talk and thoughts can be manipulated into
some useful program. They are bright and alert and learn
rapidly because they are curious about everything; they

23

can understand all aspects of a situation and it is often difficult to determine just what their position is. Once they adopt an idea, they will do anything to put it to work, even if they must hurt others to do so. They will employ flattery and even deceit to get what they want. Their memory is excellent, in some cases photographic, and their conversation is well-informed and often brilliant. They will take both sides of an argument with equal facility and, playing the devil's advocate, will lie with ease. They may appear fickle or unreliable because their dual nature prevents them from taking a stance, but they are never prejudiced or biased.

Words are the main weapon of Geminis, and knowledge of the facts is their armor. They love to argue, though if emotion enters into the argument they will become cold and abusive, because they do not trust feeling. If they can anticipate what you are going to say, they will either ignore you or contradict you. Lying is natural to them; in fact, Geminis often cannot tell the difference between truth and falsehood. They are amoral and the idea of good or evil bores them.

Because Geminis are restless, constantly moving from one idea or person to another, they tend to be superficial and shallow. They are also mental pickpockets, stealing from the minds of their associates, but, again, this does not seem wrong to them for they are as quick to scatter their own bits of knowledge as they are to pick them up from others. One Gemini cultivated a friend in order to learn his business tactics, and when he had learned all he needed to know, he moved to another state to practice them. Geminis love gossip and always listen carefully for tidbits that might be useful for one of their schemes.

Gemini is the Jekyll-and-Hyde of the zodiac. They will be cooperative and loving so long as everything goes their way, but if they are thwarted in some project, they will turn on their closest friends, for they cannot endure defeat. They become vituperative, cutting others to pieces with the one weapon they possess—words.

Love
When Gemini falls in love, he is overwhelmed with feelings of indecision and confusion. Love is always viewed in the abstract; love is something to deal with in verse and stories but not in fact. This idea of love enables Gemini to avoid the clutter of physical and emotional

ties; he much prefers to carry on an affair through letters or long telephone calls than in physical fact. A typical Gemini affair may begin through a brief meeting, on a journey for instance—an encounter that requires very little emotional responsibility and can be kept alive through correspondence, which may last for years. This allows Gemini to remain uncommitted and free, an ideal state since, like all air signs, Gemini prizes freedom.

Because they dislike being pinned down, Geminis will be impatient in the sexual act; they would rather be voyeurs than participants. No single partner can meet their demands, and they are capable of carrying on more than one affair at a time. Their pleasure in love is mental rather than physical or emotional, and thus they welcome the secret affair where meetings are difficult and mental torment is intense. The schizophrenic Geminis are bisexual, unable to resolve their preference in sexual partners, and all are unfaithful, often promiscuous.

The undemanding lover will be most successful with Gemini, since both sexes hate to be clung to or dominated. Gemini must believe that his love is greater—he likes to control the loved one, often sadistically refusing to gratify the other's physical needs in order to prove that love is an abstract notion, unfettered by bodily needs. Yet Gemini will also parade his loved one proudly, for he loves grandeur as much as his lover.

Marriage

Geminis either marry for social position or for professional advantage, preferring a partner who will make fresh ideas available to them. The male Gemini will marry an older woman who can help him; he is willing to let her enjoy his youth, which he never loses, in order to make progress on the social or professional ladder. When he has drained the cup, he will disappear on a trip from which he may never return. Gemini loves the constant excitement of travel and will often use it to escape from tiresome attachments.

The female Gemini, who relies heavily on her relationships with other people, often believes that all of her troubles are solved when she marries, that she can finally relax and enjoy her prize. But her restless nature invariably forces her to keep moving. The moment her husband becomes boring to her, she will look elsewhere for new stimulation. Geminis seldom stick with one mate through life; often they will have two and even three marriages in their search for peace and contentment, which they rarely find.

Parenthood

Gemini fathers treat their children like investments or acquired objects; they take great care that their offspring are well-dressed and well-educated so that they will reflect well on their parents. Nothing delights a Gemini father as much as showing off his child's accomplishments. If the child is beautiful—and Geminis do have attractive children—many social events will be planned so that the child may be displayed to advantage in front of friends. The child receives as much love as the father feels he deserves. The successful child is often treated like a friend or equal, perhaps even being allowed to address his father by his first name. Gemini parents encourage this kind of familiarity; it makes them seem younger.

The first stage mother must have been a Gemini. The Gemini mother parades her child before the world as soon as possible. The child is a prop to her own vanity and is often pushed into some performing art, such as dancing, singing, or acting, in order to achieve some measure of public attention and acclaim. If there has been a divorce, a child will be used as bait to attract a new husband. There is often a warm comradeship between the child and the Gemini mother. Gemini women belong basically to the world of the mind rather than the body, yet they take a perverse pleasure in showing the world that they can produce children. However, they do not thrive in motherhood and usually have only one or two children.

Friendship

Gemini makes friends easily, but he also makes heavy demands on his friends. Every new encounter is considered a potential basis for friendship and Gemini will expend a considerable amount of genuine energy to ensure the development of the relationship. But he will expect the same response from the new friend, and if the other fails to reciprocate Gemini's generous devotion, trouble will result. Gemini can be cruel and heartless with a friend he considers false, and he will quickly move on to someone new. Gemini would rather have a friend than a lover, for friendship involves less of an emotional commitment.

Because Gemini is indecisive, he will often return to old, discarded friends without realizing that his behavior might be considered fickle or changeable.

Career

Geminis are versatile and intelligent, so they are capable of doing almost anything well. But their duality often prevents them from deciding just what they want to be; they are always on the go and will hop from job to job, looking for the one that will give them some contentment. It is difficult for them to find satisfaction and they must try a number of different careers until they arrive at some all-absorbing interest in which the powers of the mind can find intellectual fulfillment. Along the way, however, Geminis will enthusiastically pretend to be everything that each role requires. Their innate sense of drama makes it possible for them to play every part to perfection, and they are often masters of deceit, living several lives at the same time. If taken to an extreme, this kind of behavior can destroy Gemini and send him into solitude and perpetual unhappiness.

The career best suited to Gemini is that of a salesman. With their verbal skill, they can talk circles around others, and their ability to lie effortlessly enables them to convince even the most sophisticated buyer. Their love of travel and their constant need for new stimulation make this kind of work attractive to their restless nature.

Gemini's love of words often leads him into the field of journalism, and the seriously intellectual Gemini is capable of becoming an important scientific researcher, an excellent teacher, or a musical composer. He can also be successful as a politician or actor, though his energy seldom lasts beyond the campaign (in which he is an excellent speechmaker), or the first night of a play. In politics, Gemini will go to any length to defeat an opponent, using gossip, scandal, and lies if necessary, and he will support whatever platform seems appropriate to the audience he is addressing. (It is no accident that the government of the United States of America has Gemini as its rising sign!)

RISING SIGNS

Gemini born near sunrise will have Gemini rising, and the description given will be exact.

Cancer rising gives Gemini's teen-age look a childish, soft innocence with very delicate features, especially the nose.

Gemini with Leo rising will be stunning, with a strong, forceful personality; he will impose his will while behaving in a generous manner.

Virgo will make Gemini more severe—neater, trimmer, less youthful in manner.

With Libra rising, Gemini is very beautiful and has a brilliant mind; an excellent combination.

The Scorpio ascendant will make Gemini a very dangerous sign, a powerful body combined with an astute mind.

Sagittarius rising will make Gemini quite tall with strong features; he will be less curious, more relaxed.

Capricorn rising will make the most mature Gemini—sincere, serious, dark, small-boned, with a sedate manner.

Aquarius makes Gemini very tall and impressive with an air of authority—a strong, confident combination.

Gemini with Pisces rising will have a less slender body with more curves; the coloring will become pastel.

Gemini with Aries rising is heavier, stronger, more mature looking; he will be athletic rather than mental.

Taurus rising will give Gemini a beautiful face; he will be slow to talk but firm in his beliefs with a sturdily built body to back them up.

CANCER

The Oedipal Complainer

June 22 to July 22

C ANCER, the fourth sign, is the second cardinal sign and the first water sign—cardinal for action, water for emotion. The animal that rules the sign is the crab, a marine animal that will withdraw into its shell at the hint of danger. Like the crab, Cancer functions on land (the present) though he hangs on to the past (water, where life originated) and will scuttle back sentimentally to the sea of emotions when he is uncertain. The symbol for Cancer, which resembles the claws of the crab, is a representation of the human breasts, the maternal symbol to which childlike Cancer clings; the pictograph is made up of two small circles (suns) each joined to a half-moon shape that looks like a cup or bowl; the cup form reflects Cancer's desire to store things, memories. The moon, Cancer's ruler, moves from sign to sign twelve times or more within a single month, indicating the changeability of Cancer and his ability to reflect whatever emotions confront him.

Cancer

The Moon

Cancer has two principal characteristics: his love of family, which always comes first, and his constant complaining about the insensitive treatment he receives from others. He is as sensitive to insult as he is sentimental.

Physical Appearance
Cancer is the weakest-looking, palest sign of the zodiac. His vitality is very low at birth, and he never quite recovers from frailty unless other strong signs are present in the chart. The head is small and the infantile bumps present on the forehead at birth continue to be in evidence throughout life. The eyes bulge out and seem to glide over objects rather than stare or gaze intently. The nose is very sensitive with small, thin nostrils. The mouth is badly shaped, with a very narrow arch that often forces the upper teeth to project beyond the lower teeth; the teeth themselves are of poor quality and the enamel is often discolored. Like suckling infants, Cancerians always have their mouths moving, with the lips drooping down at the corners.

The body is seldom symmetrical. The limbs, particularly the arms, are long and seem to hang akimbo (like a crab's claws); the legs are slender and often out of proportion to the thick-set torso. The stomach is promi-

31

nent. Cancer's shuffling, rolling gait is uneven and the feet, which turn inward, seem reluctant to leave the ground. Cancer is the poorest walker of the zodiac, with an uncertain step reflecting the changeable nature of the sign. In middle age Cancer puts on fat and has difficulty keeping his weight down, since the body tends to accumulate both water and fat. Cancer's appearance is generally untidy, like a child's. He is always staining his clothing by spilling things on himself. He does not mind this mess at all; in fact, he seems unaware of the disarray. Cancer is a prideless sign.

Personality

Cancerians are the most overtly emotional and sensitive of the water signs and must be handled carefully. They wear their feelings on their sleeves and are so easily hurt that one hesitates to touch them. If they are upset, they will withdraw in order to avoid further unpleasantness and will remain aloof until all danger has passed. It is often difficult to determine whether this is an attempt to arouse sympathy or a sign that they are truly hurt. Generally this kind of behavior is simply a means of restoring their confidence and personal equilibrium.

The Cancerian manner is quiet, soft-spoken, and shy; noises disturb him. His interest is aroused only if a subject concerns him personally, whereas abstract subjects leave him untouched and unmoved. Cancer is an introvert and tends to concentrate moodily on whatever problem involves him. He dislikes entering into conversations just for the sake of politeness, and always seems eager to return to his own private reflections while carrying on social amenities. When Cancer manages to gain power through some accomplishment, he will outgrow this phase of his nature, for most Cancerians tend to drop their shells eventually.

Cancer has a dual nature and can reverse his shy behavior and attack others like a sudden storm at sea. During such an outburst, he will reveal cunning tricks and a shrewd, grasping manner. Often the cause of this reversal will be money, since no sign, not even Taurus, loves money as much as Cancer does. Cancer also loves to pry into the affairs of others and delights in using private information to his own advantage. He has a Judas streak and will turn on those he loves if he is defeated. He is a poor loser and never stops trying to even

the score. In times of stress, he can be common and
vulgar. No sign enjoys swimming around in self-pity more
than Cancer, and often his sensitive exterior is simply a
device to hide the basic selfishness that clings to his character well into maturity.

Although Cancer is genuinely devoted to family and
home, his real love is himself. He will do anything to
acquire material comfort and affection. Though he loves
to hang on to his money, he will make a lavish display of
spending it to get love and attention, to be thought generous and affluent, to bask in the limelight socially.

Love

The male Cancer falls in love readily and becomes totally
involved emotionally. Because he has a lively imagination, he tends to dramatize his love affairs and can even
create an intense emotional attachment to someone whose
affection for him is either very slight or even nonexistent.
Cancer is extremely jealous and possessive, harboring
torturous suspicions that his lover is faithless. Since this
would be a direct threat to his masculinity, he suffers
physically, reverting to his original frailty and becoming
helpless, even impotent. It takes little to reassure him,
however, and once his self-confidence returns, he will be
caught up again in complete devotion and the cycle begins anew. Like a happy child whose toy has been fixed or
found, Cancer eagerly returns to the world of his emotional fantasy.

One Cancer man was desperately in love with his unfaithful wife, who told him that she would return to him
once she had secured sufficient money and position from
her lover. The husband agreed to her scheme and followed her to her secret meetings, which were humiliating
for him to observe. But he rather enjoyed collecting these
injustices and painful embarrassments, which gave him
the opportunity to complain about her behavior to others
whose sympathy he craved.

The female Cancer, who can be as jealous as her male
counterpart, is capable of handling more than one lover,
but being possessive, she must own them all. They are like
playthings to her, to be manipulated and moved about like
toy soldiers. Because Cancer is money-mad, the female
Cancer will drain the purse of each and every lover. She
is the shrewdest of gold-diggers and knows every way to
get her hands on money.

Cancer women are complainers and never stop crying and pleading for money and gifts like spoiled children craving new toys. They are insatiable and shop constantly, filling their closets with clothes they never wear, accumulating lovers whose emotional commitments they collect but rarely reciprocate. Their appetite for food is similar, and they will eat gluttonously all day, like babies who demand feedings every few hours. They confuse love with an emotional hunger for attention and sensual satisfaction.

The men are complainers, too, but always about the fact that they are not loved enough. Cancer will cling to his lover, and his never-ending demand for emotional fulfillment will be a continual drain. He likes to be touched constantly, as if for reassurance.

Marriage

When a male Cancer marries, he chooses a wife cautiously, generally one who is more socially prominent than he. Because Cancer's habits are vulgar and his appearance disreputable, he is often unattractive to an elegant woman, and even if he succeeds in winning her, he has difficulty in keeping her interested in him. Cancer often finds that marriage will not accommodate his unusually strong emotional needs, and he will devise clever ploys to get away from home, to pursue secret affairs. When his wife demands to know where he goes and what he does, he finds cause for complaint about her behavior, and marriage becomes a trial to both. He expects his wife to endure his demands and to provide a comfortable homelife for him; because he is obsessed with the idea of family, he is loath to divorce. He would rather remain married and complain about it than look elsewhere for another mate.

The female Cancer is equally practical about seeking a mate who will indulge her emotional demands and take care of her material welfare. When the sexual aspect of marriage loses interest for her, she will seek lovers to satisfy her emotional and physical needs, but she will cling to her husband, often enduring his abuse for her philandering. One Cancer woman left her husband for a richer man but continued to charge purchases to him, threatening to expose his tax frauds if he complained. He became infuriated and beat her, but, like a naughty child, she welcomed and even rather enjoyed the abuse, confusing it with emotional attention.

Both male and female Cancerians will look to their mates as parental figures of authority, so that they can indulge their childish whims. One marriage of two Cancerians was a perfect match. She accused him of not giving her enough money and kept after him night and day to set her up in business for herself. He placated her with promises he had no intention of keeping and complained about her constant nagging. They quarreled happily into old age, feeding on each other's emotional dependency.

Parenthood
Cancer is the true parent, the best of all the signs, because he is a child at heart himself. The father will lavish love and money on his children and become intensely involved with them. The children are given the best of everything, and they are proudly displayed and treated very affectionately in public. In fact, more real love is given to the children than to the wife. The children are a great source of pleasure to their father, who fusses over them as if he were the mother. He becomes very jealous if the child favors the mother.

The Cancer female is not as good a parent as the male. The children are usually spoiled and undisciplined. She treats them like dolls and prefers to play with them than attend to their real needs. If the child misbehaves, the mother will nag and complain until the child cries, at which point the mother will stop scolding in order to make peace. Homelife is one constant round of petty problems and emotional disorder. The children are overfed with rich, nutritionless food and overtired from daily excursions and activities. The mother will drag her children from one frivolous diversion to another, enjoying it thoroughly even when they have become tired and bored. She is an indulgent parent who understands childish ways; one day they will leave this permissive mother who spoils them but they will always remember their childhood with pleasure—it was fun while it lasted.

Friendship
As Cancer accumulates money and possessions, so he collects friends, who are regarded as possessions, to support his emotional and often financial needs. Cancer expects his friends to aid him in financial matters when necessary, and to give security and stability to his life. He privately thinks of his friends as family. Although there is a constant turnover in friends, Cancer always remains close to

those he made in childhood. If there is disillusionment, past friends may be temporarily abandoned, because they are reminders of discomfort, but Cancer always goes back sentimentally to the past at some point so that friends are never left behind for good. Anger and resentment for a friend who has failed him may last for years, but this only ensures the continuing emotional attachment he feels.

Cancer sets his own standards by the progress his friends are making. He will constantly try to keep up with them, and if a friend fails in business or in the social scene, Cancer will feel wounded, because the friend's fate has reflected on himself.

Career

Fame and extreme wealth are Cancer's highest goals and he is not content until he has achieved them. Because he needs emotional companionship, he may begin his career by joining a movement or a large organization. He will help others in a quiet way, listening patiently and working humbly, following the line of least resistance, since hard work annoys him. Cancer tires easily and usually takes the easy way out. Because he needs security, he will be reluctant to leave the larger group which serves as a protective shelter. Cancerians will jealously guard their own safety, often by secretive means of which they are usually unaware. They may even unconsciously take on the identity of another person, for their ruling moon enables them to reflect other personalities, even to the extent of mimicking voices and adopting gestures and mannerisms. They are good in business because they can change with the demands of the public, adjusting to new demands and catering to new trends. There is nothing distinctive or original about Cancer's taste and so everything he does or enjoys is reflective of popular opinion. Cancer is the consumer, the common man. The United States is a Cancer country (July 4) whose hardworking drive for success has resulted in enormous wealth. Although we have maintained sentimental attachments to the countries abroad from which we have originally come, we have also developed a kind of maternal instinct toward the rest of the world, which we strive to protect. Yet we never seem satisfied with the way things are, and there is always something—political disorder, foreign strife, social injustices, and inequities—about which to complain.

Cancer born near sunrise will have Cancer rising, and the description given will be exact.

The Leo ascendant will give Cancer a forceful personality, golden coloring, and a splendid carriage.

Virgo rising will bring order and neatness to self-indulgent, messy Cancer, giving strong lines to a sensitive countenance.

Libra will make Cancer beautiful, well-proportioned, and uncomplaining.

The Scorpio ascendant will give Cancer the power he craves as well as the forceful nature to carry it out.

Sagittarius will make a tall, amusing, more extroverted Cancer with brunette coloring.

Capricorn rising will make Cancer dark, with small features and good manners.

The Aquarian ascendant will change small Cancer into a tall, impressive person who is not sensitive but self-assertive.

The Pisces ascendant will give height to Cancer but will add to his natural shyness a self-effacing, vague manner.

Aries rising will give Cancer a strong, athletic body, an optimistic attitude, strong features, and ruddy coloring.

When Cancer has the fixed sign of Taurus rising, the eyes are lovely, the complexion clear.

Youthful Gemini rising overcomes Cancer's shyness, making him chatty, lively, and good looking.

LEO

The Prima Donna

July 23 to August 22

Leo

The Sun

L EO is the second fixed and the second fire sign—
fixed for consolidation, fire for enthusiasm. The
symbol for Leo represents two valves of the heart, two
incomplete circles (or suns), one taking power from
above and the other from within. The sun, the most powerful element in the solar system, is Leo's ruler, and Leo,
like the lion, is considered the king of the zodiac. Leo
radiates energy and vitality, and one can immediately
sense his power and authority.

Leo has faith in himself and behaves in a majestic manner
with unmistakable superiority. No one can match Leo
for generosity, but he demands exaltation in return. He
must be the center of attention, the prima donna.

Physical Appearance
The first thing about Leo that impresses the eye is the
beautifully shaped head, which is very high from temple
to crown. The oval face beams radiantly, glowing as if
from the sun, which Leo worships. Though the hair is
not abundant, it stands away from the scalp, usually in
careless disarray, like a lion's mane. The high cheekbones are narrow from temple to temple. The smiling
eyes, which eagerly greet all comers, protrude slightly and
are very keen. Leo has a high-bridged nose which reflects his sense of hauteur and his tendency to snobbery.
The lips are beautifully curved outward, and poised to
smile readily, for the disposition is sunny. The teeth are
strong and even, and the chin is firm and purposeful.

Leo's shoulders are high; the long back flows in youthful lines to very slender hips, like the lion whose hips
seem too narrow to support the huge head and fore-
quarters. Leo is not a tall sign but very sturdy with a
broad chest that makes him look slightly top-heavy and
dignified, so that Leo's lack of height often goes un-
noticed because of his sense of importance and his engag-
ing manner. The legs are short and slender, and the
carriage is the most elegant of the signs. Leo finds walking a pleasure and does it well; with head and shoulders
held high, he struts proudly and gives the appearance of
strength. The gait is even and pronounced, and it dis-
turbs Leo if others do not keep in step with him or slop
alongside awkwardly. Leo loves to show off his physical
attributes.

41

Personality

Leo has a brave heart and is both courageous and bold, especially in defending anything he truly believes in—be it friend, cause, or idea. But Leo is also willful and arrogant, expecting the limelight, the admiration of others. Leo is the true aristocrat, with a youthful, forthright attitude that is objective, open, and occasionally even naïve. He is not cynical or suspicious and has no time for those who are, preferring to use his energy to engage in whatever programs or ideas he is dedicated to promoting.

Leo's confident, smug manner irritates others because they do not understand that Leo is not limited by thoughts of failure; anything is possible for him. The secret of Leo's power over others is his underlying determination to enforce his own will; he will be bossy and high-handed in his treatment of those he considers inferior. He does not believe that all men are created equal.

It is important for Leo to make a strong first impression and he will often exaggerate to the point of lying in order to overwhelm others he wishes to impress. Leo's story must always be funnier or more meaningful, his winnings the biggest, his love affairs the most passionate. Leo loves to arouse envy but when you try to match him in any way, he will make you feel inadequate and cut you off; he enjoys alienating others, especially if he feels they have refused to pay him court or homage. No matter how unfairly he behaves or how disdainful his manner, you are expected to kowtow. If he offends you and you try to make him apologize, he will usually add to the offense before retreating. Leo can be stony-hearted and thoughtless in his resolve to be superior. If his confidence is undermined, he quickly becomes contemptuous and rigidly self-possessed. His treatment of others will be stiffly courteous but definitely arrogant. No sign can reduce another to rubble as effectively as Leo can, and he is fully aware of that power.

Because Leo is unsuspecting, he will often accept affection unthinkingly at face value and find himself the victim of an enemy's guile. Leo then goes underground to lick his wounds until recovery is quite complete. Being magnanimous, Leo will forgive but he will never again trust the offender and will treat him with an unmistakably cold hatred.

Leo speaks well; he always seems to know his subject and loves to display his knowledge. Though proud, Leo is not truly vain (unless Libra is present in the chart), and he loves to charm others and feels it his duty to entertain everyone. Leo is theater, and his most important gift to the world is his dynamic, radiant self.

Love

Leo is very dramatic about love and wants the whole world to love as ardently as he does, for he is always in love. Love ennobles Leo and makes him generous and enthusiastic. But he must keep his lover in the dependent position and will smolder if he is not exalted and adored. One Leo male would escort his girl friend, who often forgot to pay the homage he felt he deserved, to a party and leave her in an embarrassing social situation while he went off and talked to his friends; it never failed to reduce her to a state of submission. Leo women are the same way; they will browbeat or cruelly abuse their lovers to get total obedience.

With one he truly loves, Leo naturally prefers elegant and romantic forms of sex to the showy Hollywood style. To him, love is a great ideal, to be dramatized and honored. But he will occasionally employ deviate, degrading sexual practices as a sign that the lover is no longer loved, that the affair is over. He will expect the other to become disgusted and to leave him; he will not take the initiative in ending the affair on his own. Leo women use the same device. One woman, in order to end a tiresome affair, pretended to believe her lover unfaithful, a state she said she could not endure. Leo hates open argument and will not lower himself to fight. An unwanted lover is simply dismissed.

Leo genuinely believes that punishment is richly deserved by anyone who fails to love him. One man with his moon in Leo would give a lavish party, whenever he wished to discard a woman, and would brazenly fasten his attention on a new face. This would serve a double purpose—to gain a new lover and to pay off his former woman for the times she did not idolize him sufficiently. Leo does not always plan to end his affairs so carefully, often depending upon circumstances to end the attachment for him. He is too aristocratic to beg for either love or freedom, though he may employ strategies to get what he wants. Leo males will attract women as if they were sirens while the females will control and disdainfully reign over their men.

It takes Leo a long time to recover from a serious love affair; in fact he will try to avoid this kind of love so that he cannot become vulnerable to another's power. But when he has committed himself fully and generously, as he will, and then he loses, he will become aloof and distant until his confidence is regained. Empty-headed, lazy Leos desire sycophantic lovers. They use their attractiveness as a tool to gather lovers who will praise their virtue and worship their charms. Leo believes he is the only one who knows how to love and thus he feels he deserves all the attention he can get.

Marriage

Leo knows exactly what kind of marriage he wants and chooses his wife with care. She, too, must enjoy the spotlight in order to be a fitting companion for him. A good-looking woman is acceptable but she must not distract attention from her Leo husband, nor must she allow her own image to become tarnished through bad behavior. The Leo woman seeks a man who can provide her with a showplace in the community where she can play a dominant role as Lady Bountiful, the leader of this or that activity, the hostess par excellence. Her rise to social prominence inspires envy in others because it seems effortless. This is not so, however, for her strength and persistence to reach the top are boundless.

The Leo husband expects to have the whole neighborhood scrambling for invitations to his lavish parties. As hosts, both male and female Leos excel, for they prefer to have you come to them rather the other way around. When you visit Leo's home, accept what is offered and ask for nothing. Any breach of manners is considered an offense. Leo will watch your behavior carefully and if you do not match up, you will not be asked again. Nothing disgusts Leo more than a rude, ill-mannered guest, whom he considers an intruder in his home.

Leos rank high on the divorce charts. When passionate love has cooled, and the mate refuses to be relegated to the role of friend, Leo will divorce him or her without a backward glance. It is best for Leo to marry a mutable sign, such as Gemini or Sagittarius, since these signs do not mind divorce. Other signs—Taurus and Scorpio, for instance—resist the idea of divorce and will fight resourcefully to preserve the marriage.

Parenthood

If you think that naïve, childish Leo is simply a pleasure-seeker, you have been deceived. When they become parents, Leos undertake a serious program involving a good deal of hard work. Their children must be well-educated, and Leos will even go so far as to instruct their offspring themselves. Here again, pride is a determining force; Leo wants to show how talented and superior his children can be. The child of a Leo regards his parent with considerable awe. Leo may work him so hard that the child, overburdened with trying to please his parent, has little time for honest play. Both male and female Leos tax the child with lessons in manners, taste, and schooling—more responsibility than a child can bear. The child often fails because too much is expected too soon. If he can bear up, however, and achieve success, he will receive all the love that his adored parent can give.

Friendship

Leo likes young, intelligent friends, particularly those who are on their way up. He will often extend a generous helping hand or put faith in their future as if they were close relatives. Leo would like to be friendly with his relatives, but this is seldom possible, because his kinfolk often resent catering to him and the fact that this is expected of them. Leo's quick rise to success antagonizes his relatives, who often have no idea how hard he has worked for it; they see only the result and never the struggle. Leo's pride will not allow him to reveal his troubles or hardships to his relatives or friends, and he always suffers disrespect or sorrow in private.

Leo will be generous in helping a friend but he expects some return, some acknowledgment for his pains. Leo hates ingratitude. If a friend fails to repay a kindness, Leo becomes very bitter. He will also communicate his resentment toward a friend who has failed to become a success. The friend will be harassed, abused, and held responsible for this failure.

Career

Leo's enormous self-confidence and his faith in his own ability draws others to him, though his overbearing behavior can arouse their resentment. Leo's partners in any business deal must toe the mark and many close relationships have ended in bitterness when the business associate has failed to work as hard as Leo had expected. Leo will always take the upper hand, giving out orders and forcing his associates to shoulder most of the responsibilities. When it becomes clear to all that everyone else is doing the work, while Leo licks the cream off the top, taking the credit and the limelight, associates become disillusioned. Although they know they have been had, however, they recognize Leo's power and will often let the situation stand, knowing that to fight back is pointless.

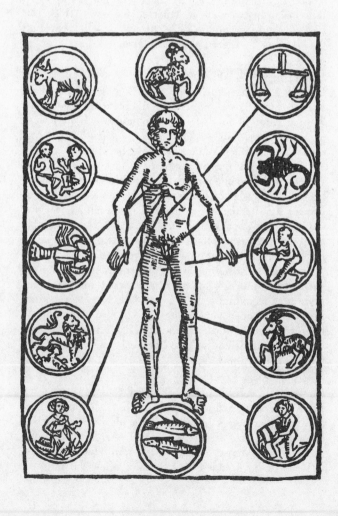

Leo born around sunrise will have Leo rising, and the description given will be exact.

With Virgo rising, Leo is slender, dark, severe, efficient, and without warmth.

Libra rising makes Leo a real beauty with strong features —a radiant, charming combination.

Leo born with Scorpio rising is no longer sunny but dark, intense, and serious.

Sagittarius rising makes Leo tall, dark, and attractive— a chatty personality, fun to be with.

With Capricorn rising, Leo loses the golden coloring and is dark, serious, very small, and quiet.

Aquarius makes Leo tall and casual, interested in others, and athletic.

The Pisces ascendant will give Leo less distinctive, fleshier features; the warmth will become cloying and Leo will be indecisive.

Aries rising will give Leo red or golden coloring; he will be ready for action, enthusiastic and patient, a good friend.

Leo with Taurus rising is solid, strong, dark, and pleasant in manner.

Gemini will give Leo a beautiful body with chestnut hair and a lovely smile—a lighthearted personality.

Cancer rising gives Leo a fair complexion and makes him shy though friendly, concessive, and kind.

VIRGO

The Censor

August 23 to September 22

V IRGO, the sixth sign, is the second mutable sign and the second earth sign—mutable for adaptability, earth for practicality. The symbol for Virgo is the virgin, a human figure, and the pictograph represents the female generative organs, closed and untouched. The traditional zodiacal image shows the virgin bearing a sheaf of wheat, indicating the harvest or the gathering of material needs. Mercury, the ruler of Virgo as well as of Gemini, is the planet of reason and intellect; its symbol combines the cup of the moon, which rules emotion, the eternal circle of the sun (energy and will), and the cross of matter, signifying practicality. Mercury, through reason and emotion, enables man to express his practical ideas.

♍︎

Virgo

☿

Mercury

Virgo is the sign of discrimination, selection, and criticism, and he likes to judge and shape events and people. Virgo loves work and the rendering of services to others; in fact, Virgo is the workhorse of the zodiac, perceiving only the present and its needs and setting about to put everything in order. Virgos think of themselves as perfectionists but one must be perfect to please them; this so-called search for perfectionism is really only an excuse, however, for them to censor and criticize the efforts of others.

Physical Appearance
Superficially Virgo resembles his mutable sister Gemini and the first general impression is attractive until closer scrutiny shows up various flaws. The head and face seem unrelated to each other, for the cranium is disproportionately larger than the facial region. The veiled eyelids seem to reduce the size of the eyes, which are too close to the nose, and dart about trying to observe everything at once. The nose is wedge-shaped and straight. The lip, from lip line up to the base of the nose, is very long and clings to the teeth. It is the longest upper lip of the zodiac, giving severity to the overall facial expression. Although Virgo smiles often, the face lacks warmth, and the smile seems automatic and forced. The bridge of the nose has a very narrow curve, and the face is very narrow with a weak, receding chin. The complexion is not clear but the general appearance is clean and neat.

The body is quite straight, lacking curves, although the

stomach is often protruding. The women can be either statuesque if tall, or thin and stiff like a caricature of a schoolteacher. The feet are small and one often turns inward, giving the walk a labored appearance.

Personality

Virgos are very quick about everything they do, and are always poised and ready to be analytical and critical. They size up others rapidly, making immediate judgments of their worth. They enjoy being tactless in pointing out any mistakes or failings; this seems to establish their superiority over others and give them the advantage. The Virgo nature is competitive. Nothing excites Virgo so much as the opportunity to test the wit or knowledge of a well-known expert or celebrity by asking difficult, carefully prepared questions.

Though Virgos can be ingratiating and attentive, always on time, and efficient in planning parties, they hate social demands and come off badly in a social setting. They lack personal grace and style, but they affect an obsequious manner and can be successful in hiding their social awkwardness, at least while they are on the make.

Virgos are basically servants and it is difficult to establish a truly equal relationship with them. One never feels able to trust them completely. Their cynical, cold nature is always evident; they do not know how to be honestly warm. In their quiet, respectful, hardworking way, they will climb coldly from one stepping-stone to another until they reach the top; they are yes-men until they become the boss.

Virgos are jealous of others, resentful of their abilities and accomplishments. It delights them to take others down a peg either in fun or for a serious purpose; they are expert in detecting the vulnerable spot in other people. For example, Virgo makes a fetish of being neat, and always looks freshly scrubbed and brushed, not casually so like Libra, but deliberately polished. He enjoys staring down anyone else who is not as well-groomed and likes to make the other feel somehow dowdy and inferior.

Virgo is petty and it pleases him to have a real reason to criticize another. He will cultivate superiors, learning all of their personal traits, and later he will use this knowledge as a weapon against them. Virgo loves gossip and uses it well. He has one perpetual aim—to use everyone—and you are kept on his list as long as you can be used to his advantage. The moment Virgo feels there is nothing you can do for him, you are openly betrayed and dismissed, no matter how kind, considerate, or faithful you have been. Nasty things will be said about you behind your back, as if to justify Virgo's betrayal of you. Insecure Virgo has built up a new ego by diminishing yours.

Virgo does not give the impression of being vain, but do not underestimate his petty, servile ways. He wants to make history and will climb over others to make it. Nothing can stop Virgo; he is relentless. For example, notice how a Virgo will cut into a conversation, cleverly turn it to a subject in which he is interested, and keep it there. Virgo only listens for his own purposes; anything else bores him. To please a Virgo, talk about his work, his programs, his goals, his interests. No sign is as single-minded on the subject of himself as Virgo.

Virgo is ungrateful and treacherous. He will knife anyone who has been good to him and is contemptuous of anyone over whom he has triumphed. His sly nature is such that he cannot believe others are honorable enough to be worthy of trust. Virgo uses words cleverly but he has a mean streak and delights in making up cynical phrases to fit each of his friends and associates. He hates to hear others tell success stories and will not hesitate to dismiss such a storyteller as the purveyor of worthless trash. The Virgo mind is full of hate and hostility caused by jealousy, and a Virgo will eliminate anyone no longer useful to him. Elimination, as in the intestinal tract which Virgo rules, is his natural function, and he will take a sadistic pleasure in getting rid of people.

Love

When Virgo falls in love, it is purely for sex. The lover must be able to satisfy Virgo's considerable sexual needs. Each new image arouses sexual desire, but so long as you can remain sexually attractive to Virgo, you will retain his love. The slower you are in yielding your gifts, the longer you can keep an affair alive. Nothing is more unattractive to him than easy surrender, which stamps you as cheap and worthless.

Virgo can be either chaste or promiscuous, one extreme or the other. There are many spinsters, one-man women, and confirmed bachelors in this sign, but there are also the chasers who frequent bars or pickup joints in the search of a one-night stand. This type of Virgo can be quite degenerate in his sexual appetites. One Virgo man, for example, allowed his wife to bring home men she didn't know. He would enjoy watching her perform with the stranger; this aroused him enough to make love to her himself.

In spite of all this, Virgo probably ranks lowest on the scale of sexual prowess. He is not romantic except as the chase itself is romantic. Sex is something to be done as quickly and efficiently as possible.

When Virgo says he or she loves you and behaves in a jealous manner, do not be flattered. This usually simply means that you are serving some useful role for them and are considered a piece of their property. Anyone who tries to lure you away is depriving Virgo of a useful tool —no more. For both male and female Virgos, true love is not involved; they are never tender or sympathetic unless there is something they cannot get without showing affection. A Virgo man likes to make his lover carry out useless but time-consuming chores for him so that her mind is completely involved with him.

Marriage

When Virgo sets out to marry, he will consider only someone with money or position and one who will please his relatives. He is always on the lookout for good health in a potential mate, because this is one of his concerns, particularly in terms of good diet. Virgo's mate must be helpful in supporting his ambitions. Nevertheless, Virgo lacks vision and often makes the wrong choice. Although he will try hard to make the marriage succeed (since he hates to be wrong), he will gladly get rid of his spouse if there is no hope. One Virgo man used the confidante of his wife, who had left him, to keep him informed of her love affairs. He pressured the confidante constantly, taking a kind of masochistic satisfaction from hearing information that was humilating to him. It soon became clear that he could never restore his marriage, and in order to get rid of the confidante, he told his wife that the confidante had betrayed her, thereby dismissing both women at once.

Virgo women marry men who can support them, since they do not need love. They will go from one husband to another until they get as much as they want. One Virgo woman married four times. Although she looked battered and wrung out she relentlessly worked the social circuit and managed to get herself a man before her reputation had reached him. Her diligent and prideless labors and her desire to eliminate old husbands served her well. Virgo is not sentimental so divorce does not bother either sex and they never have regrets.

Parenthood

The Virgo man has few children unless he marries a Cancer or Scorpio, who thrives on motherhood. Virgo is not excessive in showing affection to children any more than to a lover. The children are given good diets and their health is attended to; they must appear clean and neat and their report cards must be excellent. Virgo is not clever in knowing how children should be treated, and caring for them is more of a chore than a pleasure. Virgo finds it safer to remain aloof from children than to become involved and appear inadequate as a parent. Virgo parents do not like to ask others, even professionals, for help or advice about their children, who are considered a private matter.

Friendship

Virgo tends to deal with his friends in terms of certain categories into which they are placed immediately. Virgo acts like a professional interviewer when he first meets someone, putting the person through a form of interrogation even in a casual situation. One Virgo man I know goes so far as to write down answers to his questions for future reference. Virgo women are the same and are always asking such questions as, "What kind of hair spray do you use?" "Where did you get that beautiful dress?" and so on. You are constantly on a witness stand providing Virgo with information that enables him to determine your potential worth to him. If you are in a particular profession, Virgo will tap you for information, such as a piece of legal advice if you are a lawyer, a free diagnosis if you are a doctor. One doctor's wife had to warn a Virgo hostess that her husband would walk out if a medical question came up, since the hostess had made a habit of asking the couple to dinner just before her all too frequent trips to the hospital.

Food, like good health, is always a Virgo concern. If a Virgo is after your friendship, he will wine and dine you, expecting, of course, that you will sing for your supper. The business lunch was probably invented by a Virgo; he loves to eat but he hates to waste time.

Virgo likes to have friends with imagination and charm but the most important quality is professional position, whatever that might be. As a friend Virgo cannot be trusted, and if he fails you in an emergency, you can take it as a warning that you are losing ground with him. Virgo cannot be counted on to respond emotionally to a friend. If you should encourage him to share a personal problem of your own or to give you advice or assistance, he will turn icy. It is a satisfactory relationship for Virgo as long as you are being exploited, but when you try to reverse the role, Virgo shuts off.

Career

Virgo is always at work and he works hard, so he can be a valuable asset in business. Everything he does has a purpose and he is always going about his work even in a social situation. He is efficient and orderly and knows the details of every operation, since he has a petty mind. He will not hesitate to point out to his boss where something has gone wrong, even if the boss has made the mistake. Because he is good at sizing up people and has no hesitation about firing people who don't measure up, he makes a perfect personnel officer. However, he has his mind set on a higher position where he can wield even more power. He makes himself invaluable to his superiors by serving them well, but once he makes it to the top he can be ruthless in dealing with underlings, for he has been one himself.

Though Virgos can shine in almost any kind of business, they (particularly the females) are often involved in health programs or hospital work, because of their concern with health. One Virgo woman who worked for a doctor learned about all the drugs and treatments he used. When the doctor refused to give her a raise, she encouraged his patients not to return for treatment and took another job, this time for a woman skin specialist from whom she lifted formulas so that she could go into business for herself. With her clever application of the information she had stolen from her former employers, she also managed to steal their patients. Her ambitions did not even stop there. She visited an astrologer and took copious notes during her visit. Although she does not know even how to set up a chart, she gives phony readings to the same clients to whom she sells her stolen formulas and treatments.

Virgo born near sunrise will have Virgo rising, and the description given will be exact.

The Libra ascendant makes a tall, well-dressed Virgo with good manners and beautiful eyes.

Scorpio rising will increase Virgo's desire for power, making a heavy, severe, formidable type.

Virgo with Sagittarius rising will be tall, warm; he will like to talk and inform others rather than pilfer ideas.

The Capricorn ascendant adds dignity to Virgo's working habits; this will be a tiny, symmetrical, well-mannered individual.

Aquarius makes the strangest Virgo; a tall, cool, friendly individual whose behavior is very contradictory for no reason.

Pisces rising will make Virgo's features pale and indistinct; the body will be heavy and lumpy; the personality will be vague.

The cardinal signs such as Aries give enthusiasm, warmth, and an athletic build; this Virgo will be less scheming than usual.

Taurus rising will give Virgo a sweet, pleasant manner, pretty eyes, and a good complexion; the personality will be much softer.

Virgo with Gemini rising will have a youthful personality and will be chatty and friendly, with a clear-complexioned pretty face.

The Cancer ascendant makes a kind, sympathetic Virgo, whose body is pleasantly curved; this type will invite you to dine.

Leo rising gives Virgo stature, generosity, and a radiant appearance.

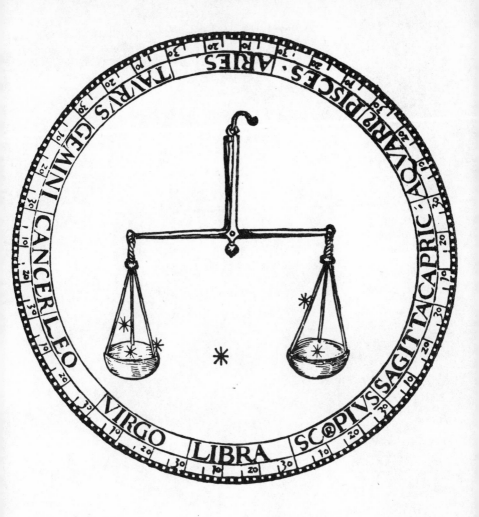

LIBRA

The Narcissist

September 23 to October 23

Libra

Venus

L IBRA is the seventh sign of the zodiac. It is the second air sign and the third cardinal sign—air for intellect and cardinal for action. The symbol for Libra is an empty scale, which, unlike the other symbols of the zodiac, is an inanimate object, neither human nor animal. This indicates that Libra is without a life of its own, that it needs constant stimulation from the outside in order to function. Venus is the ruling planet for Libra as well as for Taurus, which accounts for Libra's sociability and beauty.

Librans are doers, not thinkers, and along with their good looks, they have easygoing dispositions as long as they get what they want. Yet Libra can be the most ungrateful sign of the twelve and it certainly is the vainest—hence the term *narcissist*.

Physical Appearance

The most distinctive features of the Libran are the eyes and the wide jaw. The eyes are large and wide open. The complexion is consistently clear and the hair is fine and silky though thin. The shape of the face, because of the well-defined bone structure, is markedly even in feature and line. Calm and peaceful, it is the most beautiful face of the zodiac. The head is quite large and the jawbone is as wide as the brow, sometime wider. The nostrils are delicate, and one will often flare higher than the other. There is usually an indentation in the center of the forehead and a swelling at the temples. The teeth are even and the front two teeth often have a wide gap between them; this separation becomes wider as the Libran grows older. The mouth is the largest on the zodiac and seems wide enough to extend to the outer sides of the cheeks.

The Libran body is graceful and athletic and there is a constant urge to exhibit its beauty. Female Librans are never breasty but the hips are very wide. The thighs are symmetrical but the legs are lanky. The feet are extremely large and bony—sometimes this is the only ugly feature of the body. The torso in both male and female is slender, long, and never fat.

Personality

Librans are conscious beauties, never unaware of them-

61

selves or any attribute of their bodies. There is no particular passion or warmth in their manner because they
use their attractiveness to obtain whatever it is they need
or crave. They constantly flirt in order to involve others
with themselves, not because they want others but because they need others to want them. Librans have good
manners even when they are shy. Their voices are quiet
and they speak slowly. The vocal range is low when
normal but will rise into bell-like tones when excited.

Librans are very well-dressed, for their bodies must be
properly adorned. They can somehow appear chic in the
simplest attire and their sense of color and line is generally excellent. A Libran will express himself in a distinct, individual style of clothing and many are well
known in the fashion world for this trait. Since they care
more about their looks than any other sign, they spend
the most time and money on all forms of body care, in
order to avoid aging. They do not have to be clever or
sophisticated to be aware of style and correct appearance,
but the more sophisticated they are the more time they
spend searching for clothes and for ways to remain
beautiful.

If you think this smacks of self-love, you are right. The
sign is the incomparable narcissist of the zodiac. Their
narcissism is constantly at work and colors every department of their lives. To be loved, admired, and wanted
is their obsession. Your love must be constant and never-
ending, or they will become unnaturally depressed, for
they cannot understand why they have been abandoned.
Their demands are excessive, not out of love for you but
because they parasitically feed upon the love you bear
them and get their strength from it. They are like empty
vessels that need a continual supply of adoration to restore and revive them. This kind of greed for attention is
often found in political demagogues who encourage
mobs to swarm around them; Adolph Hitler had Libra
rising and loved to hear the cries of hero worship that his
presence caused.

Librans have no pride and cannot accept the truth
about their true nature. The crowd that surrounds and
applauds them is all the assurance they need of their
worth.

Their superficial, easy manner indicates a lack of
strength. Indeed, they are often called the "beautiful but
dumb" sign. They are rarely intellectuals, unless Virgo

or Scorpio is also found in their chart, but they are shrewd, sly, and self-protective. They dislike involvement in anything outside themselves. They hate arguments, which will tax a shallow mind and will expend emotional energy that they do not have to spare. They are clever at hiding their parasitical nature: though they are takers, not givers, they will often give beautiful presents to cover up their true intentions. They will cultivate others for various reasons—material gain, social advancement, or nourishment for their professional ambitions. They are natural promoters and will often use insidious means to achieve their ends. But the struggle to achieve these ends must not last too long, for Librans have the lowest endurance of the twelve signs.

Love

Librans work hard to keep lovers coming and going. At first they will give you constant attention until you are completely involved but soon the demands of keeping up the love affair will become too much for them and you will become part of the background. Librans will never relinquish their lovers completely, for they may be needed again. The primary function of a lover is to amuse, satisfy, admire, and exalt Libra, and if you are easily won, the excitement is blunted. If Libra is rejected, he becomes completely demoralized; he cannot believe that anyone could weary of him, though he does nothing to deserve love. Yet even when sorrowful, Libra will immediately seek to dispel the blow by filling the environment with new people—or he will renew the campaign by reviving his original charm until you surrender. In failure, he is without pride, and nothing will compel him to look within himself for any failing. A male Libran who was deserted by the one he loved exclaimed, "I feel so sorry for her for giving me up"—and he meant it!

Surprisingly, Libran vanity in the male is even more profound than in the female. One male Libran I know invariably becomes furious if his date is better dressed and gets more attention than he. All Librans are very competitive and will often scheme to humiliate their loved ones. It is always a shock to learn that Libra can be spiteful, for he seems so blandly unaware of his offenses to others.

One would expect Libra, with all the beauty and impeccable manners of the sign, to be capable of only the most sophisticated forms of lovemaking, but in fact Libra enjoys and practices the most extreme forms of sexual expression to gain satisfaction. Librans often have a prurient fascination with sex, though like the other air signs (Gemini and Aquarius) they require a great deal of stimulation to become aroused. In many Librans, the sexual act itself can be a nuisance and though all sorts of methods may be employed to arouse and be aroused, there is often little personal interest or involvement. Libran females can be remarkably clever prostitutes. Their indifference is reassuring to men; they are attractive to escort in public, artful in bed, but need no commitment.

Because Libras give so little real emotional commitment to a lover, it is not surprising that they like to talk about their affairs. By comparing and weighing the attitudes of themselves and their lovers, they can remain uninvolved and even dissipate whatever interest they may have had in the loved one. Libra likes orderly endings to love affairs. This is to their advantage because, remember, they may need to call on the discarded lover at a later date.

Marriage

Librans marry and divorce more than any other sign; as in love affairs, the same partner becomes a bore after everything has been gleaned from the relationship. If Libra stays married, it may be purely for physical comfort because he is too lazy to seek elsewhere. He may even have become impotent, or inertia—Libra's worst malady—may have set in. Libra's greatest fear is loneliness; he constantly needs someone to lean on in order to keep that scale in action. He lacks inner resources, and he cannot bear to think that he is unwanted and unloved.

The male Libra usually marries a woman who is not as attractive as he is, hoping that a plain woman, undistracted by her own vanity, will be willing to give more. He also feels that a plain woman is likely to get less attention than himself. It is not unheard of for a handsome Libran to marry a nagging woman; the constant prodding and pushing is a reassurance of love while the abusive scolding satisfies his somewhat masochistic needs and keeps his interest alive. A completely adoring wife is treated with contempt and thought unworthy.

For the female Libran, a husband is the one who pays the bills. The marriage of convenience suits her best.

She often does well in the marriage market because of her surface attraction, but she is actually cool and unemotional. She is always after something—a house, a fancy car, a trip around the world—and she loves to circulate socially, climbing from one relationship to another. She enjoys being on the best-dressed list or considered the most accomplished hostess in her circle. She likes a man who is never at home to intrude on her constant scheming but out in the world making money to pay for her social successes.

Marriage is Libras' career and they are masters at it. They will patiently ignore their mate's shortcomings so long as they are supported, cared for, and allowed to indulge in their pleasures. More attention is given to the comfort and beauty of the home than to the mate, for pleasant surroundings are necessary to their happiness.

If the mate should become boring or, worse, if the mate should want the divorce in order to marry another, Libra's spiteful and vindictive traits come to the fore. The end of a Libran marriage is usually a financial disaster. The rejected female Libran will do everything in her power to strip the man of all his resources and then she will put him quite completely out of her mind; he will simply cease to exist. One Libran woman, who was at a party, found herself being watched quite intently by a male guest. When asked by another guest why she was being stared at, she could not think of a reason. Finally, the man came and spoke to her. When he moved away, the other guest asked her who he was. She replied: "I think he was my third husband. I scarcely remember him."

Parenthood
The Libran mother or father is the most permissive of parents—not for love of the child but for freedom from the child's problems. They abhor the idea of discipline for it involves argument, reasoning, or emotional expense. The children of beautiful Libran mothers are always badly raised and often spoiled or even bought off. They can do and have anything they want as long as they do not become a nuisance. However, the child must always reflect well on his parents by wearing the finest clothing and attending the best schools. The Libran parent wants the child to look handsome and to display good behavior. The child is used for social advantages, and the parent lacks real interest in him. This is not because the

child is unloved but simply because there is no time in the busy Libran schedule to devote to the child beyond the supplying of essentials such as food and clothing. The Libran mother has her card games, club meetings, social schedule, political rallies, or career. The Libran father is too busy promoting his business ventures.

Friendship

Libra's constant turnover in friends is caused by his extreme ingratitude, for he will treat a friend thoughtfully only while he is getting what he wants and dismiss the friend afterward. But Librans are superficially popular, and they like to accumulate friends. They expect everyone to help them realize their ideas and support their interests, but they do not treat others the way they wish to be treated. Librans will ignore or drop friends who are not interested in their projects. Librans often seek inferiors whom they can dominate; they do not like to be outshone. Because they are not thinkers, they need concrete proof of friendship rather than a simple sharing of ideas or pleasures. They are constantly trying to make up their minds as to whether it is wealth, status, or the approval of their friends that they really want.

Activity for Librans is vital, and they are great partygoers. They are naturally magnetic and gracious. Since they must be doing something—anything—at all times, they keep in touch with life by being with others. They hate to read, but they always know what is going on in the world by their continual social contact.

Career

The male Libran is a promoter and con man; he can promote more ideas that never come to fruition than any other sign of the zodiac. Game playing and clever planning are his strong points, but true obligations of all kinds irritate him. Personal pleasure must always somehow be tied up with a "big deal." Librans have the poorest memories of the twelve signs, so that the means by which a business transaction is to be consummated are forgotten. Librans hate to pay bills, and leaving debts behind means nothing. Spend they must, for they are the spendthrifts of the zodiac, but once the pleasure has dissipated, they resent anyone who tries to collect his due. Charge cards must have been invented by a Libran.

Librans may appear to be listening but they do not

hear what you tell them; it is often difficult even to get their attention. Concentration, particularly on anyone else's problems, is painful, exhausting, irritating. But they love to talk about themselves, their own schemes, and will often talk others into supporting their vague ideas. They enjoy putting others to work on their deals, dominating and bossing them, but if success and money are slow in coming, they will move quickly on to another source of income, often missing out on the winnings. Librans lack vision in business transactions; they want to spend lavishly for immediate returns but have no pride in admitting failure and starting anew. Bankruptcy does not bother them; it is simply one of the hazards of the business world. The Libra/Scorpio combination can produce a financial wizard who will build a fortune by outwitting the gullible. Scorpio schemes and is persevering, while Libra plays the game with enthusiasm and without being afraid of hurting others.

Strangely enough, Librans are interested in law and politics, but only as a means to social or public prominence. They love having influential contacts who admire them for their position, and they will devote whatever emotional energy they have to attaining status and money.

Because of their innate sense of style, Librans can also be very successful in the fields of art, graphic design, dancing, theatrical work. Without Virgo or Scorpio in the chart, Libra isn't particularly creative himself but he is expert in applying surface attractiveness to another's original ideas.

Libra born near sunrise will have Libra rising, and the description will be exact.

Scorpio rising will darken Libra's complexion and make the body strong and heavy; the face will become mysterious looking and the eye will be veiled.

If Sagittarius is rising, the Libra will be tall, elegant, and beautiful, an athlete with the chic of a jet-setter.

The Capricorn ascendant will make Libra a serious brunette, small in build and conservative in personality.

Aquarius rising will make the most stunning Libra, who will be a humanitarian.

Pisces rising gives the Libran features a soft, indistinct, dreamy look with starry eyes; the symmetrical lines of Libra will be lost.

The ascendant Aries, the opposite sign to Libra, will make the features of the face flatter, less positive, and the body more athletic.

If Taurus is rising, the body will be heavier, the bone structure less prominent, and the facial features strong and pleasant.

If Gemini, an air sign like Libra, is rising, the body will be youthful and move with a graceful flow and easy manner—a great beauty.

Cancer will give Libra sensitive features and a tendency to be overweight.

Leo rising will make Libra quite short, with proud bearing and a small body and high head.

Virgo rising will narrow the Libran body and weaken the face; the body will be tall, classically proportioned, and controlled.

SCORPIO

The Sex-Obsessed Demoralizer

October 24 to November 21

S CORPIO, the eighth sign, is the third fixed sign and the second water sign—fixed for relentlessness, water for intense emotion. Scorpio has three symbols to represent the three distinct types born under the sign. The first pictograph (top right), standing for the lowest order of Scorpio, represents both the generative organs, which Scorpio rules, and the scorpion, who carries a death sting (sarcasm) in the tail. (According to Sumerian mythology, this symbol represents the spermatozoon.) The second symbol (middle right) is the eagle who flies high above the earth into the sun; this is the evolved Scorpio type who displays brilliance in the realm of the intellect. The third symbol is the dove of peace, a symbol of love often seen above the altar in Catholic churches, the highest Scorpio of all (Gandhi had Scorpio rising, for instance). All Scorpios are obsessed with power, and these three symbols reflect the ways in which Scorpio obtains it: through emotion and instinct, through intelligence, and through love. One of the reasons for the complexity of the sign is that it is ruled by two planets —Mars and Pluto. Mars is a fighter and strikes on impulse. Pluto, also a very strong planet, is forceful and magnetic and always operates on a large scale—as a powerful ruler or perhaps a gangster, king of the underworld.

Scorpio

Mars

Pluto

Scorpio has the worst reputation of the zodiac. It is a power-hungry sign, obsessive and relentless, particularly in its mania for sexual experience, through which it can demean and demoralize those who fall under its control.

Physical Appearance
Scorpio is the most easily identified sign. Scorpio's prominent features are a large beaklike phallic nose, built for attack, and a heavy forehead with bushy eyebrows that often meet over the bridge of the nose. The head is the strangest and least attractive of the zodiac: the head goes straight up, narrowing almost to an egglike shape at the crown. The hair grows in a tight, kinky curl but is sparse and the male Scorpio will eventually become bald; even the female's scalp can be seen through her hair as she ages. The brow has a distinct hardness of the look of death. Scorpios rarely show emotion in the face,

though the nostrils will flare if they are moved or angry. The eyes recede under the brow, hooded with slanting, Oriental lids that droop down at the corners until the eye is almost covered. The sharp, piercing gaze locks itself on both persons and objects; it is difficult to look away from Scorpio's intense stare. Even in laughter, the eyes never smile but hold their detective stare. The cheekbones and jaw are tightly clenched, reflecting Scorpio's invincible nature. The teeth are set so closely together that it looks as if there were no separation between them; they are usually of poor quality and color. The lips are fleshy, and the inside development often turns out in a snarling fashion. The complexion is murky with a gray pallor.

Scorpio's shoulders are hunched and heavy; the fleshy back seems to dominate the body. The torso is top-heavy and thickset, perched on muscular thighs and legs, which give the body a loose-jointed carriage as if everything were out of coordination. The body is often asymmetrical and many Scorpios are bowlegged. Older Scorpios have large stomachs, for they are greedy and have voracious appetites. The heavy buttocks lie flat against the body. Yet, for all their clumsy walking habits, Scorpios are fast, even agile, and often make fine athletes. Scorpios' movements are decisive and deliberate, and their bodies seem to give them personal pleasure. There is an overwhelming self-satisfaction and exclusiveness in Scorpio's appearance.

Personality

Although Scorpio is the most totally selfish sign of the zodiac, it is also the most magnetic, invariably compelling the attention of others and inspiring awe, even fear. The characterstics they project are cynicism and a domineering will, which discourage familiarity. Scorpio is crafty and cunning, understanding the weaknesses of others as well as their strengths. At first he will ask what seem to be harmless questions but he files away every response for later reference, like a detective compiling clues. Since they remember every word, every story, Scorpios are a bottomless pit of stored information; they are very resourceful. Their manner is effortless and cool but under pressure they become remorseless and cruel.

Never tell Scorpio a secret for it will be used against you if he feels it necessary to do so. Scorpios will seek explanations for anything they do not understand and ferret out any information they think they might need. They are capable of building a case against anyone; they are the FBI agents of the zodiac—the women as well as the men. If you are in no way useful to them, Scorpios will not go to these lengths since they do not like to waste time. They are too aware of their power to spend time with useless people, but their natural instinct is to probe into and investigate everything. Their minds are very practical.

Scorpio is a sign of extremes. Like all fixed signs, Scorpios are either exceedingly polite and polished or strikingly crude and vulgar. Some Scorpios enjoy telling jokes to degrade and embarrass those whom they wish to attack. Scorpios can be very jealous, so you should never tell them of your successes, for they will think of many ways to slight you and diminish your accomplishments. They would rather pity others than envy them.

Love
A Scorpio man is too practical about human relationships to fall deeply in love; his real love is power and making his reputation secure through wealth and position. Whatever is left over will be given to a lover. Both male and female Scorpios are always discontented in love and complain constantly about the loved one, usually that they are not loved sufficiently. A Scorpio often feels that his lover is weak and inattentive, and unable to appease Scorpio's voracious appetite. Scorpio does not hesitate to tell the world about his lover's weaknesses, but if the lover should be unwise enough to expose Scorpio's inadequacies, he would be making a costly mistake. For a love affair to run smoothly, Scorpio's loved one must be submissive with no life of his or her own; the lover must allow himself to be absorbed body and soul. But no matter how much is given, the lover will always be treated ungratefully.

Scorpio has no interest in his partner's responses or satisfactions, only in his own, for Scorpio is the most selfish sexual sign. His famous sexual appetite is like his eating habits—greedy and intense. He cannot be distracted from his own pleasure during the sex act for otherwise he will fail to achieve a climax. This points up the fact that Scorpio—reputation aside—is really weak and lacks sexual strength. Perhaps this is because Scorpios give so much thought to their sexual obsessions that their energy is dissipated by the time the real thing comes along.

The Scorpio woman comes off better sexually for she can project a strong sexual image and attract men without having to display any particular prowess. The Scorpio woman is both predatory and amoral; sex is treated as if it were a job to be done, nothing more or less. She does not have to love a man to sleep with him; there is no real tenderness or affection expressed during the sexual act.

Though it is deceptive, the extreme sexual attractiveness that Scorpios have is powerful. They are physically as well as mentally magnetic, emitting a kind of sexual emanation and often a strong musty body odor. Scorpios always look a little damp; even in cold weather they seem to be perspiring. Their anxious, imperative nature seems to aggravate the glandular flow.

Both male and female Scorpios love to quarrel, which is an important part of lovemaking. Fighting seems to stimulate them, and the troublesome atmosphere they create seems to make things exciting for them.

Scorpios resent needing others to satisfy them, and this results in hostility and anger, a passion to degade or demoralize the loved one. Many Scorpios believe that love interferes with their rise to power and they will often torment anyone who threatens to involve them. Many Scorpios are pimps. They keep their women in a subordinate, degrading position by holding out the promise that one day they will enjoy sex together. This never happens, of course, for Scorpio's own sexual inadequacies would become evident, and he would lose control over her. He creates an atmosphere of sexual power, but this is fabrication.

Marriage
Both male and female Scorpios prefer mates who will allow them complete dominance, who will endorse everything Scorpio initiates. A partner who agrees with, praises, or approves of every expression of Scorpio's drive for power is the perfect choice, for any interference would destroy the relationship. In return, the mate receives comfort, support, and protection. But he or she must forget about self-esteem; any attempt toward self-improvement is belittled and the mate's opinions and ambitions are treated with contempt. Scorpio must keep his mate nameless and free of outside distractions in order

to have her completely at his disposal. With the submissive mate, Scorpio can be devoted and loyal, though failure in any way will incur his hatred.

One Scorpio husband, a nondrinker, would encourage his wife to drink in front of guests, all the while making disparaging remarks about her drinking. His abuse would eventually drive her to tears and when she had become completely submissive, he would rush her to bed; he required her surrender to enjoy her sexually, and this involved giving her friends the impression that he was married to a hopeless drunkard. A Scorpio wife I knew enjoyed tormenting her husband by creating violent scenes involving vicious physical attacks. She wanted to make him suffer because he would not allow her to dominate the household. Both male and female Scorpios can be relentless nags; every failing or weakness in the mate will be noted and added to the list until a big fight is inevitable.

Parenthood
The powerful Scorpio father subdues and demoralizes his children; he is never satisfied with their behavior and is always disappointed by their lack of accomplishment. He does not understand them, particularly if they are at all sensitive. Eventually they will run away, and though Scorpio will suffer in private about this, he cannot help himself. If the child is somehow successful, yet submissive and adoring at the same time, Scorpio's emotional commitment to him will be intense though they will never be close. The Scorpio father is unable to feel sympathy for his children and cannot give them the confidence they need. He prefers to remain aloof though his authoritative demands will be felt; the child must either succeed or escape.

The Scorpio mother is rather more sympathetic to her children though she is also demanding. So long as the children are under her control, she will be fiercely loyal and protective.

Friendship
Scorpio is very discriminating in choosing his friends, and once he has offered his friendship he feels entitled to criticize any weaknesses or failures. If a friend resents this, Scorpio is invariably surprised. Friends will be chosen for their usefulness, for the performance of various services. Scorpio will give a great deal to a

friend at the beginning as a kind of insurance against the day he expects a return.

Because Scorpios are easily aroused to anger, which subsides very slowly, they are dangerous enemies. They are troublemakers, and if you do not do their bidding, they will ride roughshod over you. They demand constant attention and complete loyalty. Scorpios will find many ways to keep your attention riveted on them alone, until you are exhausted and drained. They are the vampires of the zodiac. They feed on people and transform this sponged-up energy into success and power at the expense of their victims. They are magicians.

A Scorpio is always concerned with his own health and that of his friends. He is deeply touched by the death of a friend and is always helpful in times of illness. When his own health is bad, he will expect to be looked after in the same way.

Career

Scorpio begins every new venture by expending every effort to obtain a position of importance. Scorpios make themselves useful to others, willingly offering their energy or time, in order to make their way to the top. This cooperative attitude is a sign that you have something Scorpio wants—information, advice, connections, and so on. Scorpio expects his business associates to work equally hard and to produce exactly what they promise. If they fail, Scorpio will harass them until the promise has been kept. It would be a great mistake to make a contract with a Scorpio and expect to get away with short measure.

Because Scorpio likes to outwit others, he is good at making business deals; he is resourceful and can accomplish jobs that many others would find impossible.

Because he is a natural detective, Scorpio can be valuable in pointing out defects in any system or weak points in any organization, though he rarely has constructive criticism to offer. He understands the uses of power, and he can make people cringe. He is capable of running a large corporation.

His energy and attention to details, coupled with intelligence and a cool manner, make him a good doctor, especially in surgery. Scorpios are also powerful warriors and leaders. But if they are not on the right side, they can also be destructive criminals, leaders of the underworld, and successful gangsters.

Scorpio born at sunrise will have Scorpio rising, and the description will be exact.

If Sagittarius is rising, Scorpio will be scholarly, intelligent, and have an easy manner; the body will be tall.

The Capricorn ascendant diminishes the forcefulness of Scorpio and makes a small, well-mannered type that assumes responsibility gracefully.

Scorpio with Aquarius rising will be tall and thin, with a less intense personality not motivated by power.

When Pisces rises, Scorpio is more concessive, lighter in coloring, and more willing to serve others.

The cardinal Aries ascendant makes Scorpio a great game player whose drive is to win; he will have a fair complexion and a good athletic build.

Taurus rising will make Scorpio more pleasant, more sociable, and better looking.

Gemini rising will ease out Scorpio's forcefulness; Scorpio becomes younger looking, an interesting talker, and more socially agreeable.

The Cancer ascendant makes Scorpio kind, sympathetic, affectionate with children, and attractive.

Leo rising will give Scorpio a lighter coloring and a more generous, kindly manner.

Virgo will make Scorpio even more scheming; these individuals are small, stern, and endlessly busy.

Libra rising will give Scorpio great beauty and good manners—a good combination for social success.

SAGITTARIUS

The Don Juan

November 22 to December 21

SAGITTARIUS, the ninth sign, is the third mutable sign and the third fire sign—mutable for adaptability, fire for romance. The symbol for Sagittarius resembles an arrow but is a pictograph of a leg, from the thigh to the knee, the part of the body ruled by the sign. The planetary ruler is Jupiter, whose symbol is composed of the crescent moon, which represents the consciousness of the soul, and the cross of matter. Because the moon is higher than the cross, the consciousness is instinctive and the emotions are purified.

Sagittarius

Jupiter

Sagittarians believe they are the great lovers of the zodiac. They move rapidly from one person and one idea to another, loving all. They are very permissive with others, but they expect the same treatment; they must preserve their freedom from involvement at all cost.

Physical Appearance
Sagittarius has a tall, symmetrical, well-proportioned appearance. The face is long and well-formed; the brow is high and narrow from temple to temple. The nose is also long with well-shaped nostrils that flare slightly. The generous mouth has full lips that curve upward into a heart-shaped smile. The teeth are strong, large, and of good quality, with the centrals protruding slightly forward, not unlike a horse's teeth. The eyes are large, dark, and kind. The chestnut or dark brown hair is full and abundant; Sagittarians have more hair than the other signs.

The body has wide shoulders, a long back and narrow hips that flow smoothly into the most beautiful thighs of the zodiac. Sagittarius's height is mostly in the thighs. The feet are graceful and the carriage is lithe. The gait is easy and athletic, with a Spanish flavor (Spain is a Sagittarian country). The sign of Sagittarius rules travel, and every journey a Sagittarian takes is a pleasurable exercise. The bone structure is prominent and is never obscured by fat. The large bony hands are gentle and delicate. Many Sagittarian women are small but well-proportioned with a quick, generous expression and the same breezy good looks as the male. The body never seems to be in complete repose. It is always ready to move, and if a Sagittarian is careless with his appearance, he will seem disjointed and his carriage will appear slouchy and undistinctive.

Personality

Sagittarians can be noble, refined, and forceful, but their first instinct is to spring away at the slightest pressure, as if they feared their inability to live up to the impression they give others. Sagittarians are gamblers; everything is a game to them and the spirit of adventure enters into the simplest activity. They are masters at bluffing and they are often extremely lucky. In order to get what they want, they will promise anything, meaning what they say at the time but eventually changing their minds.

They want to be liked by everyone. They are constantly driven to obtain the good will of others, to be considered a good fellow, but they will waste much time in seeking approval from people of little consequence, so afraid are they that someone will be overlooked. The simplest gesture of approval is enough to reassure them that they have won over another person. They rarely take the effort to turn an acquaintance into a real friendship. Superficial relations are enough for them; they are essentially flirtatious—with ideas as well as with people. They thrive on ideas of every kind—travel, theater, art, law, and so on—and they are constantly in search of new areas to explore. They are tireless in the pursuit of their ideal, the goal of happiness, but they follow up every lead they come across on the way.

Sagittarius distrusts security and frets when he feels confined and safe. He is extroverted, extravagant, and rash—taking chances with everything from money to health. He is so charming that he is quickly granted forgiveness, which he accepts as a license to do it all over again. But he is so self-oriented that he cannot understand why others should find him unreliable.

Sagittarians have enormous faith that they will eventually find the right track to run on, and once they do find something that satisfies them, they will commit themselves and settle down happily. Until that goal is achieved, however, they are uncomfortable in a single place and have no inner peace.

Love

Sagittarians fall in love at first sight and idolize the image of their loved one. From then on, they are making love to an ideal, rather than a real person. Even when they are in love, however, they can easily fall in love with another, for there is always some new feature to attract them. They are incorrigible flirts and each new conquest reinforces their behavior—but they never know when to stop. They collect lovers indiscriminately, often becoming involved on impulse with worthless people.

Sagittarians are unreliable lovers. Most of their energy is devoted to courting a new lover, while keeping the rest dangling on a thin thread. Their light, tentative touch simply reflects their emotional shallowness, although it is attractive to many people. The fear of intense lovers who might trap them has taught Sagittarians to use the device of treating the lover as an idol, so that they can maintain a distance and prevent close involvement. Because of their Don Juan mania to conquer all, Sagittarians rarely become completely committed in a pure, deep love affair.

Sagittarius, the fire sign, is too shallow, irresponsible, and romantic to be truly emotional. But he cannot tolerate inconstancy in others; he is conceited enough to believe that a lover will continue to love him forever, though the lover may be neglected or even forgotten. Sagittarius is not cruel, but foolish.

Sagittarians cannot endure an intense sexual relationship, preferring to sample here and there. The sexual act is not as important to them as the courtship; in fact, Sagittarians will have many lovers to hide the fact that sexually they are second-rate. They will prance like horses in a show ring, displaying their charms for their own sake, not as a seductive promise. One male Sagittarian travels a great deal with his luggage full of pomades, shaving lotions, smelly bottles of musk, and every beauty aid on the market to help him preserve his charms. He even goes to Switzerland regularly for hormone injections to keep him young and handsome. When he has a party he invites all his woman friends, and they usually mill around waiting for him to select one of them. He will pick one while the others circulate around him, trying to attract his attention; it is like a circus with the host as ringmaster.

Sagittarians never grow up. One male in his seventies, who has been in the hospital several times, never stops flirting with the nurses; he genuinely believes they find him attractive, and all his stories are about how many women—waitresses, secretaries, clerks—are crazy about him. One Sagittarian woman delights in flirting with all of her friends' husbands at parties, laughing and joking about meeting them at some indefinite time in the future. She feels she is the life of the party, but she is unconcerned with, even unaware of, the embarrassment and unhappiness she causes.

Some Sagittarians are bisexual. They often take great pleasure in playing their men off against their women, knowing the confusion it creates because they cannot be pinned down to one or the other.

Marriage
Male Sagittarians dodge the wedding ring for as long as they can, for they are born bachelors. They are only caught during the first heat of an affair. Once the step is taken, they refuse to change their ways and continue to act as if they were single. If the marriage goes bad, and it often does, they move on to a second and third. They are gamblers, remember, and always looking for a better bet, next game.

The only way a Sagittarian will stay married is if he or she is allowed complete freedom. The mate must be permissive and tolerant. If a Sagittarian husband fails to turn up for dinner, or if he turns up with a collection of friends picked up on the way home, his wife must be uncomplaining and prepared to cope. Sagittarians may even disappear for days at a time. They often deal with insults, disagreements, or any painful situation by traveling. One Sagittarian wife, upset over some complaint her husband had made, got up one morning, packed a bag, and left for Europe. Her husband couldn't locate her for a full month but she did return—without any explanations.

This irregular behavior can break up a marriage if the mate does not understand or condone, but can also make the domestic scene one of constant excitement. It is usually best for a Sagittarian to marry another Sagittarian, since each would accept the other's desire for freedom.

Parenthood
Sagittarius shows little honest attention to the child, who is often thought of as a romantic symbol or asset, the result of lovemaking, to be fussed over and enjoyed when

the spirit moves him. A Sagittarian's usual generosity The Don Juan
does not involve spending time with his offspring; he
counts on relatives or even friends to care for his children's needs. One divorced Sagittarian father was told
that his son was seriously ill; he made no effort to visit
the child, saying that he had to make a business trip. He
did not want to be tied to the bedside of an ailing child.
Though Sagittarian fathers can be lavish in bestowing
gifts, they are usually selected by friends or business
assistants.

Even the Sagittarian mother will avoid caring for her
children if she can find someone else to do the work. She
will adore them, admiring their good looks and achievements, and giving presents and spurts of affection, but
she cannot sustain her interest in them from day to day.

Friendship
Sagittarius is often closer to his friends than to his lovers,
because friends make fewer demands and are satisfied
with only occasional attention. Friends are often more
important to him than the mate. Sagittarius is more loyal
to friends; he would be willing to lose a mate or lover
before he would part with a friend. Like all fire signs,
however, Sagittarius will quickly bolt if he feels hemmed
in by anyone. He does not argue, he simply disappears.

Career
Because Sagittarians are always looking ahead to the
future, they enjoy forecasting, and they have more vision
and imagination than most signs. They make good lawyers
because they understand the law and are clever with
words. They are often writers, though they write with an
eye toward posterity rather than for their contemporaries,
and they make good priests or ministers. They love ideas,
and spiritual philosophies and religion fascinate them.

In business, Sagittarians are good gamblers and often
make successful deals. But they do not like the responsibility of administration. They prefer to travel, spreading
goodwill for the company, or to smooth over personnel
problems, since they are open and sympathetic to others.
As soon as they begin to feel stuck in a job, they will
move on to another one, even in a different field altogether.

RISING SIGNS

Sagittarius born near sunrise will have Sagittarius rising, and the description given will be exact.

The Capricorn ascendant will make a most serious, small Sagittarian who is genuinely interested in others.

Aquarius makes Sagittarius unusually handsome and interesting; this individual is very tall with outstanding features and a kindly manner.

Pisces, the water sign, will soften Sagittarian features, making the individual heavier, lighter in coloring, less gregarious.

The cardinal sign of Aries makes an athletic Sagittarian with golden coloring—an exciting, warm personality.

The fixed sign of Taurus will make Sagittarius quite heavy, less talkative, more reserved, but good looking.

Gemini rising will give Sagittarius smaller features, a very pretty smile, and lovely manners.

Cancer will make Sagittarius short, heavy, fair, sensitive, less talkative.

If Leo is the ascendant, the radiant generosity added to Sagittarius's kindness makes this a handsome, charming combination.

Sagittarius with Virgo rising will have less generous features and will be more severe and businesslike.

Libra rising makes the most beautiful Sagittarius of all —a graceful, well-dressed individual with lovely eyes.

The Scorpio ascendant makes Sagittarius much more important, reliable, and solid—in appearance as well as manner.

CAPRICORN

The Honor Seeker

December 22 to January 20

CAPRICORN, the tenth sign, is the fourth cardinal sign and the third earth sign—cardinal for performance, earth for practicality. The Capricorn symbol is a pictograph of the human knee; the circular form on the right is the kneecap. This is the part of the body that enables man to stand upright and to climb; like the goat, Capricorn is surefooted and steady even in high places. The ruler of Capricorn is Saturn, which is a factual, sober, austere influence. The symbol for Saturn is a combination of the cross of matter (practicality) and the crescent moon of consciousness below it, indicating that facts weigh down the soul.

Capricorn

Saturn

The most serious and dignified of the cardinal signs, Capricorn is very concerned with his reputation. He is deeply ambitious but quietly persistent while achieving his goal, full of conviction that he is right and determined to present his exalted self-image to the rest of the world.

Physical Appearance
Capricorn has the smallest skeletal structure of the twelve signs. The head is small, the hair very silky but not abundant. The brow is narrow from temple to temple. The eyes are dark brown, sharp and penetrating, and the space between the eyes often has deep vertical lines. The nose has a goatlike spread, protective yet inquisitive. The mouth is generous and seems too serious to smile. When the smile does come, however, it is surprisingly beautiful, showing strong white teeth. The neck is slender and the chest is narrow. The torso is small with narrow hips; thighs are slender and the leg is very well-shaped from the knee down. Capricorn has the smallest ankle of the twelve signs. The feet are very small but beautifully formed. The walk is unique; Capricorn takes such great care in placing his feet exactly in the correct position that they seem to have a will of their own, both swift and sure.

Capricorn is the most self-conscious sign; the manner and carriage are dignified and well bred. The females are ladylike, and there is a distinct air of importance and propriety in the males. Capricorns are embarrassed by familiarity and levity, since these characteristics threaten to disturb their dignity. They do not like to be seen without clothes.

Personality

Capricorn seems unapproachable at first. Yet once his confidence is won, the self-protective air lessens and a quiet warmth is apparent. The initial diffidence results from Capricorn's inner doubt that he can be interesting to others. Though he is self-centered and has an extremely high opinion of himself, he is without vanity. His general appearance is serious and vigilant because he is distrustful of others, even suspicious—particularly with those who try to make friends too quickly. Time is of the greatest importance to Capricorn, and he expects everything to run its natural course, without hurrying. Once a rapport is established, however, Capricorn will do everything to cultivate and develop a close relationship. He will continue to test others to reassure himself of their worthiness.

Capricorns are high strung and tensions will build up when impediments arise, though nothing can discourage them from attaining a goal once they have set their sights on it. Capricorns are reliable and dependable in pursuit of a goal, but they tend to put ambition ahead of personal relationships, which can be swept aside if necessary. Capricorns can develop strong dislikes, even hatreds, if any people or events conspire to keep them from their chosen path. They do not like new ideas or surprises but tend to be very conservative; since they respect time, they exalt tradition.

Capricorn wishes more than anything else to be honored and will dedicate his whole life to bringing the world to honor him. He does not seek fame—in fact, he scorns it; anyone can get his name in the newspaper—but he wants to be considered a figure of distinction. Capricorn will employ humble tactics, waiting patiently and working toward the moment of exaltation.

Capricorn is the most opinionated and self-centered sign of the zodiac, and he believes that no one can be more correct than he. It is unforgivable to slight or demean a Capricorn; it is considered a blow to his self-esteem. He can forgive being lied to, being deceived, or taken advantage of; in fact, he expects it since he has a low opinion of human nature. But it is utterly devastating for a Capricorn when a disrespectful act or a blow is leveled against him and it may take years for him to recover. Capricorn is a vindictive sign and can wait patiently until the time comes when he can even the score. Scorpio will plan his revenge, but Capricorn believes that the opportunity to exonerate evil will simply and surely come in good time.

Love

Earth signs are never thought of as having a sense of romance, nor are they given credit for knowing or caring much about love. Taurus pursues money, Virgo is busily managing and supervising, and Capricorn is organizing the show and achieving his ambitions. But in actual fact, Capricorn does care a great deal about love, which is often a source of inspiration to him. Capricorn is probably the best sexual performer of the zodiac, though his quiet manner and desire for privacy often hide this considerable talent from view.

Both Capricorn males and females seek a mate who is capable of fulfilling their voracious sexual appetites, which occupy much of their attention. The goat is traditionally a sexual beast. In Greek mythology the lascivious satyr has the head, chest, and arms of man and the legs, horns, and ears of the goat. Goats have also been used in the past to symbolize Satan—the hero of sorcerers and witches. Capricorn can display both traits—understanding of evil and its uses, and abandonment to sexual excesses.

Capricorn males select their lovers with great care; they are not flirts in any sense of the word and do not like to waste time in searching for a lover. They know by instinct when they have found the right partner. The sexual act is often a kind of ritual for Capricorn, not simply the fulfillment of a need or a form of release. He expects and is capable of quality lovemaking. The male is an expert, a connoisseur in love; he seeks to achieve total satisfaction for both himself and his partner through his innate desire for the highest form of sexual love.

Because Capricorns take time in finding the suitable lover, in seeking physical and emotional security, they remain faithful and rarely end an affair or marriage. They have much to give a lover; silly, romantic gestures bore them. If they are deceived or abandoned, they will usually turn their energy to their career and become very difficult to deal with on a personal level. They can be contemptuous of anyone who refuses or mistreats their love. If they do not find the right sexual partner or mate, they care for no one who is not useful in furthering their ambitions.

The female Capricorn is the most unfortunate woman of the zodiac. She too seeks to be exalted in love, but because she tends to select men whose ambitions she must support, she is never truly satisfied. She is more generous than the male Capricorn, but she is rarely lucky in love. The unattached Capricorn woman is usually involved in her own ambitions, in pursuing a career that will bring her the honor and position she craves. She can be cold and scheming, using her sexual power to seduce men and get control of them. They are sometimes nymphomaniacal but are practical enough to use their drive to achieve what they want.

As they are masters at lovemaking, so Capricorns are masters at hating. One of their favorite ways to show hate is to curse people. I remember two sisters, one a Capricorn, the other a haughty, proud Leo. The Capricorn sister needed some money. When she asked her younger Leo sister for a loan, the reply was, "I neither borrow nor lend to anyone." Capricorn was furious and said, "You've always been selfish and greedy. The day will come when you won't be able to speak because God will have taken your tongue." Some time later, the younger sister fell and hit her head, suffered a stroke, and went into a coma for nine days before she died. During her last days, the older sister sat by her, begging her to speak but getting no response. The ironic twist of the story is that the younger sister was never able to tell where she had put her savings, so Capricorn was never able to find the money.

Marriage

Male Capricorns make ambitious marriages, usually for professional or social advancement, finding someone else —always in secret—to provide sexual satisfaction. They are always climbing and will go on to a second marriage, but only if they must. Their conservative nature and sense of dignity do not condone divorce lightly.

Because Capricorn is self-centered, he is often unaware of his cruelty to others. If he loses the support of his mate, through death or divorce, he will withdraw into a rigid stance, being unable to shift easily to another. Misfortune will dog him. Capricorn in this position can be a truly tragic figure.

One famous advertising man dropped his first wife after becoming affluent, and she died of a broken heart watching him turn into a social lion. His parties were the highlights of the holiday season until a handsome man attending one of them fell in love with his second wife and took her away. He has achieved considerable success in life but spends it quite alone with no one to honor him. Older Capricorn men will marry women younger than themselves, preferably attractive and ambitious girls whose strength will restore their own youth. They do not care if their young wives lie to them, so long as they are respected, honored, admired.

The female Capricorn wants to be kept and always seeks a wealthy husband, though she is rarely successful in this, even if she is particularly beautiful or intelligent. She will take on a series of silly lovers or spend all her energy on a career outside the home if her marriage is unsatisfying to her. The female Capricorn does not like other women, though she generally has a long list of women friends whom she uses constantly. If her marriage is successful, she will remain faithful, though it is her husband's position she is protecting.

Perceptive men can sense the covetous, self-seeking Capricorn woman and they tend to avoid her, even though she would do anything for her man. They seem to know she wants to control them, to trap them into dependency.

Parenthood
Capricorns have few children, which is fortunate, for they are often mistreated. The father is too busy pursuing his career to pay much attention to his child, and he expects the mother to handle the discipline and whatever affection might be necessary. He will provide the necessities but no attention or love. His child, like his car, will be kept in running condition and will be considered a useful asset but not an object of loving indulgence.

The Capricorn mother is not much better. Her sons will get whatever attention she can spare. Her daughters, however, are treated like servants and are burdened with household chores and abused if they do not behave. They are humiliated if they show any interest in their own projects, for the mother's jealousy makes her unable to tolerate her daughters' doing things for themselves. One divorced Capricorn mother neglected her daughter and spent all her time in another city with a young lover. The girl failed in her studies and had to leave school. The mother pretended she could not understand and ignored the girl. When the mother married again, a man with two sons, she took an interest in the boys and spent time and affection on them. Her daughter is severely neurotic but she pretends not to notice.

Friendship

Just as Capricorn comes off rather shabbily in marriage (unless the moon, ruler of the marriage house, is well-placed on the chart), he does not fare well in friendship. He seeks friends who have power, believing that this will assure him of a safe future, a way to the top. At the beginning Capricorn can be a devoted friend, serving loyally to prove his sincerity. But, as a poor judge of human weaknesses, he gives too much at the start of a friendship and then suffers when it goes wrong. Many bitter misunderstandings and quarrels result when Capricorn feels that his devotion has been abused. He will become cynical and begin to suspect all his friends of double-dealing. He will put his friends on trial and expect them to prove their trustworthiness again and again. Nothing is so damaging to Capricorn than to know he has been deceived. Once a lie or false move is detected, a friend may be tolerated but under no circumstances may he be trusted again. Some Capricorns can be good friends, but usually they are on guard, waiting for some deception, some breach of trust.

Time enters into every aspect of Capricorn's life, and he is a master at judging when to bring about retribution. Although not as dangerous as Scorpio in disposing of his enemies, there is often a severe fate in store for anyone who has wronged Capricorn. He can wait for years, watching his enemies progress through life and compiling evidence against them; he believes firmly that he will live to see them swept aside and that, when the time is right, they will fall from grace, disappear, or even die. A case in point is Richard Nixon, who finally attained the goal he sought so ardently for years and who believes that—as another prominent Capricorn once put it—"all those who doubt me are stung with absurd remorse."

Career

Capricorns are organizers. They like to keep records and they honor company traditions. They also like to follow plans and will work tirelessly and ploddingly to see that they are carried out. They know that time and patient effort will pay off eventually. Capricorn likes to do his duty; he sees it as a trust, as the right thing to do. When he is praised for his accomplishments, he accepts the honor unquestioningly.

Capricorn is not a backslapper, and he is not socially

graceful like Sagittarius or Gemini. He prefers to work quietly and seriously behind the scenes, though his ultimate ambition is to be on top, to be in a high position where others may share his own exalted image of himself and pay the homage he feels is his due.

RISING SIGNS

Capricorn born near sunrise will have Capricorn rising, and the description given will be exact.

Aquarius rising makes a tall Capricorn with fair good looks; this individual will be famous and popular.

The Pisces ascendant makes an unimportant Capricorn, vague in coloring, indecisive in manner, but kindly.

Aries will make Capricorn well built, strong, fair, outgoing, and generous.

The fixed sign of Taurus gives Capricorn a more positive quality—he is sturdier, quieter, friendlier.

Gemini will dilute Capricorn's appearance; this combination eliminates his drive for power, and he will be easy to know and fun loving.

Kind, sympathetic Cancer will make Capricorn sensitive, soft-spoken, inclined toward overweight.

Leo rising gives importance and authority to Capricorn; this is the most confident Capricorn.

The Virgo ascendant makes Capricorn a hard worker, slender, and quick but petty and ill-mannered.

Libra rising gives Capricorn lovely eyes and manners with flawless skin and a sociable personality.

Scorpio rising gives Capricorn assurance, power, purpose; he will be dark, tall, with strange eyes—a real history-maker.

The Sagittarius ascendant makes a tall, handsome, jovial Capricorn with a generous smile and a sincere manner.

AQUARIUS

The Fame Freak

January 21 to February 18

A QUARIUS, the eleventh sign, is the fourth fixed sign and the third air sign—fixed for unyielding resistance, air for intelligence. The symbol for Aquarius resembles the wind disturbing the waves, but is a pictograph of the ankle in motion, since Aquarius rules the ankles. The ruler of Aquarius is Uranus, which is symbolized by a combination of three forms: two crescent moons (consciousness), the cross of matter (practicality), and the circle of the sun (energy).

Aquarius

Uranus

Aquarius desires to deal with the problems and hopes of all humankind; he is concerned with the life of the community rather than the individual. But he must always be in the spotlight and will do anything to attract public attention, no matter how freaky or perverse.

Physical Appearance
The Aquarian has a large, domed head. The crest of the head is high and wide, the forehead is wide and square-shaped. The well-defined bone structure gives a large, well-planed face, and there is often a hollowness to the cheeks above the jawline. It is a distinctive, craggy face. The neck is slender and the shoulders are broad. The back is large and long, the hips are wide, the legs bony, and the feet large. Aquarius is the tallest sign of the zodiac.

Personality
The first impression that Aquarius gives is that of openness, a friendliness with no particular emotional content. Sweet, cloying people are abhorrent to Aquarius and nothing surprises him more than to find that they inspire emotion in others, which he finds annoying. His manner is offhand and he is not easy to get to know. The general attitude is that of extreme independence; Aquarius is casual, indifferent to approval, not concerned with making an impression. The cool, detached behavior can seem brusque but it is effective as a protective device to prevent involvement before Aquarius feels ready to accept it. Emotion frightens him and he alienates anyone who tries to force a relationship. This is all because Aquarius has little interest in individuals; he is involved rather with life as a whole and with the future of mankind. He has no real interest in his own personality or in the per-

sonalities of others. This makes it easy for him to alienate or cut off other people without a second thought.

Aquarians are egocentric, contrary, and perverse. They refuse to be forced into any responsibility or any role that infringes on their freedom; they prefer to be uncluttered by people or objects. Their private nature makes them seem heartless and they can be cold as ice, even cruel, enjoying the discomfort of anyone who interferes with their privacy. Aquarius is the strongest air sign, depending almost entirely on intellect, and the Aquarian seems to have a psychic power, an ability to see into the future while discarding the physical realities of day-to-day existence.

Aquarius is the most spiteful sign of the twelve. Aquarians enjoy belittling others with casual insults. They love to argue, diminishing the self-esteem of their opponents by ignoring their arguments or dismissing them as unworthy or overemotional. They love to annoy conservative people, whom they find boring; anything that reeks of respectability is a target for their often deadly wit. They relish the opportunity to attack another's naïveté or lack of sophistication. They love to shock, and they often do since their behavior tends to be eccentric.

Aquarians will work hard at instituting reforms and will make an earnest effort to eliminate waste and ignorance, but they can also become extremists and radicals, fanatically involved with their ideas. They will neglect everything else to put their ideas into effect, and they can be destructive if any impediment crosses their path. If, however, a single flaw in an idea becomes evident, they will suddenly drop it and go on to something else. Aquarians tend to become involved with groups in order to put their ideas across. They count on their friendly manner to win them supporters, but one wrong word or disagreement will send them running. In spite of their breeziness, they are contradictory and often difficult to get along with.

Aquarian females are usually the worst offenders, hogging the limelight whenever they can. They do not distinguish between notoriety and true fame and will jump aboard any bandwagon or adopt any political viewpoint if it promises to attract attention to themselves. One particularly eccentric Aquarian became the producer of a Broadway show that had not been properly publicized; after he took it over, he managed to make it a success. But he pushed aside the talented authors and the

director as if they did not exist and took entire credit for
the show's success, accepting all the honors. He was
neither creative nor very imaginative, and this was his
first taste of fame. He began to believe everything he read
about himself in the papers and from then on, everything
he did was calculated to get as much publicity for himself as possible.

Love

One cannot expect a smoothly running love affair with
an Aquarian, who will become bored with a lover as
quickly as he falls in love. Everything is done in extremes.
Relationships will start off with a bang, and you will be
given undivided attention until the excitement wears off.
At that point you will be dropped without ceremony if
the initial feeling can never be revived. You will be
treated like a stranger as soon as the affair is over unless
you are clever enough to transform the relationship into a
form of friendship. The male Aquarian makes a better
friend than a lover.

The female Aquarian is domineering and likes to run
the affair, making all the rules. She can be a heartless
virago, pressuring the man into submission until not a
shred of his self-respect is left. If he manages to escape
her, she will be prideless and masochistic in pursuing him
until he returns. Perversely, she will find the lover more
precious if he does not want her. Aquarian women often
have masculine mannerisms, and many are lesbians.

Aquarians will carry on one affair at a time, concentrat-
ing on one lover until they become tired. They do not
like to take the responsibility for ending an affair but if
the lover doesn't get the hint, they will provoke a quarrel
or create an impossible situation so that the lover will
have to leave.

Both male and female Aquarians grow to hate any
lover who wants them more than they want the lover. An
Aquarian woman I know makes a practice of fastening
her attention on any man at a party who is clearly involved with another woman, and the unattached men do
not attract her at all. The men, too, always want their
best friend's lover or mate; any woman belonging to another man provides a stimulant. Even a homosexual
Aquarian male will behave this way—by sleeping with
the wife of a friend, he is able to establish a relationship
with the man.

Treat an Aquarian badly, disappoint him, break appointments, keep your emotions hidden—he will be captivated.

Marriage

It must have been an Aquarian who originated the idea of common-law marriage. The legal tie is distasteful since it represents limitation of freedom. Even after accepting a ring, the Aquarian resists the restraints of marriage. One Aquarian wife used to introduce her husband by saying, "Meet my husband; he is married but I am single." An Aquarian husband, because he likes to come and go as he pleases, will make few demands on his wife; she is free to do as she likes. Though this would please another Aquarian or a Sagittarian, many signs cannot accept this kind of open marriage.

The Aquarian wife is less lenient than the Aquarian male and will become jealous if she feels her husband is having more fun than she is. She would not be hurt by his infidelity, only envious of his good times. Aquarians are not moral, and immorality does not bother them— only its occasional inconvenience. An Aquarian wife knew that her husband was flirting with her grown daughter by a previous marriage and though she said nothing to him, she simply sold her house and moved into a small apartment, so that her daughter would have to find a home of her own.

There is another side to Aquarius, however. Some Aquarians are downright prudish where sex is concerned. As a mental sign rather than a physical one, Aquarius is not much interested in the sexual act and it often takes some kind of unusual stimulation to provoke a response. Aquarius is the most quarrelsome sign of the twelve, and Aquarians sometimes like to torment other people. Harangues between husband and wife are endless, and they are often carried on in the presence of friends. These quarrels can take the place of sex or other kinds of physical involvement. After a verbal storm, a peaceful period will be enjoyed until another agonizing fight comes along.

Parenthood

The child who has an Aquarian mother or father has a good friend. The father likes to play games with his child and take him on trips. The child is a pal. There is little discipline and no rules to be obeyed, and serious problems are ignored. The child who needs advice or guidance will get only half-serious answers. Yet the father will confide in his child, sharing his own problems, unmindful of the fact that the child may be emotionally or intellectually unable to cope with them.

Aquarian mothers have little patience in caring for their children and will often leave the responsibility to others. But they will take full credit for their children's successes, basking in the limelight with them. They will also expect to be taken care of by their children when they are too old to support themselves or to attract husbands. But they are unsentimental and, for example, if a child runs away from them, they are not offended. Aquarians have an ungrateful streak and they assume their children have the same, so they feel justified in neglecting responsibilities.

The child of an Aquarian parent should be happy to settle for a casual friendship, for the parent who knows how to be a friend to his own youngster is rare. While such a relationship may not be altogether appropriate or satisfactory when a child is young the rewards will come when the child has matured.

Friendship

Aquarius rules the eleventh house, the house of friendship, and much interest and energy are given to cultivating and keeping friends. Aquarians start out, as in everything else, with a tremendous burst of enthusiasm. Friendship for an Aquarian can be a joyous adventure, but it can also be a source of information and aid. Aquarius is interested in all the new ideas a friend may have to offer and will often begin a friendship by asking questions of a casual nature. Aquarians are not suspected of exploiting their friends, because they seem to be interested in higher goals, but they do not hesitate to use friends when necessary or convenient. The egocentric Aquarian will make any idea his own and will resort to argument or guile to force a friend into giving him the information he needs.

The friend will gradually realize that Aquarius has become the dominant partner, that he has imposed his will and has taken control; this process is slow and casually carried out so that it is difficult to perceive and even more difficult to escape. Aquarians are clever at putting their friends under an obligation; their demands seem natural and harmless. The female Aquarian, for example, will drop all of her troubles in your lap by flattering your ability to understand and advise. No one's problems will seem as important or as immediate as hers. But you will find a number of other friends who have been given the same confidence and responsibility.

The moment you ask an Aquarian for his help with your own problems, you are told to ignore them, that they will go away. You will be told not to take yourself so seriously. A friend of one Aquarian lost her sister after a long illness. She went to her friend, weeping over her loss, and was told, "Stop being so dramatic. You look terrible when you cry, so stop it and think about something else!"

Aquarians can be deceptive and elusive if they feel you need their friendship more than they need yours. You will feel that you have been tricked into feeding their egotistical demands. Your ideas are no longer your own; they belong to Aquarius and you are expected to sit by quietly while he claims full authorship. If you make any attempt to point out your contribution, Aquarius will create a chaotic scene or quarrel that will confuse everyone and everything.

Career
Aquarians are humanitarians only in an abstract sense. People are not as real to them as ideas, ideologies, and sociological concepts. The eccentric do-gooder holding forth on all the injustices done to mankind is usually an Aquarian. These Aquarians tend to display the very trait they despise most in others; they will use their power to control people and to insist on their ideas in an unyielding, insensitive manner. They enjoy the applause they receive as great humanitarians.

Aquarians find it very limiting to stick with one company, one group, or one movement for very long. Their energy is considerable but it is limited and tends to come in bursts. They are perfectly suited to working in large organizations; they do not take things personally and they work well with others so long as they are given a certain amount of freedom. They can be creative and inventive but they must not be confined or limited.

They are better suited to intellectual than physical work and they can be good writers because they love to spread their ideas to large audiences. They love being famous, and they are happiest writing about themselves rather than anyone else. (Norman Mailer is an Aquarian.)

The most famous Aquarians of all have been either in

the arts (or some form of creation) or in government. In both fields they can gain the limelight for their mental achievements by transcending the everyday world and dealing with change, reform or orginal ideas on a universal level.

RISING SIGNS

Aquarius born near sunrise will have Aquarius rising, and the description given will be exact.

If Pisces rises, Aquarius becomes amenable, soft, self-effacing, and lighter in coloring and heavier in appearance.

Aries will ease up Aquarius's determination. These people are fair, athletic, quick to make friends, generous, and kind.

Taurus rising will make Aquarius short, dark, and heavy; the personality will be hard to know but generally charming.

Gemini diminishes Aquarius's unpredictability; this personality is adaptable, friendly, and fun.

When Cancer rises, it softens Aquarius into a more sympathetic, sensitive personality; the body will be short and heavy.

The Aquarian with Leo rising is willful but sunny in personality and aristocratic in manner.

Virgo rising makes a stern, busy Aquarian, less of a fighter and more of a businessman.

The Libra ascendant makes a graceful, beautiful Aquarian with lovely eyes and good manners.

Scorpio rising will make a powerful Aquarian who is awesome and hard to know and get along with.

The Sagittarian ascendant makes the most attractive, most generous, and least determined Aquarius.

The Capricorn ascendant will make Aquarius dark, small, well-mannered, thoughtful, and respectful.

PISCES

The Spiritual Panhandler

February 19 to March 20

Pisces is the twelfth sign of the zodiac, the fourth mutable sign and the third water sign—mutable for amiability, water for emotion. The symbol for Pisces resembles two fishes tied with a band of limitation; this represents two crescent moons (consciousness) held back-to-back by a horizontal bridge that symbolizes the material world. The symbol also represents the two human feet, which support the whole weight. The body is dependent on the strength of the feet—if they are weak, the body is weak. Neptune, the planetary ruler of Pisces, has the trident as a symbol; the cup of the moon (consciousness) speared through by the staff or cross of matter (materialism) from which is suspended the circle of the sun (spiritual energy). Neptune is a mysterious planet, the sponsor of dreams rather than daily realities.

Pisces

Neptune

Pisces is a dreamy sign and its outstanding characteristic is vagueness and indecisiveness, which Pisceans can turn into an appealing helplessness designed to obtain your support and sympathy. They are the beggars, the panhandlers, of the zodiac.

Physical Appearance
There are all shapes and sizes of Pisceans, just as there are all shapes and sizes of fish, from the tiny minnow to the great whale. The hair is usually the same color as the complexion, pale and washed out. The head is not large but there is a swelling at the temples; the forehead is low. The eyes are either very starry and blue or watery and expressionless. The nose is large and puttylike and clings to the cheekbone. The cheeks are jowly and hide the bone structure. The mouth is large, the lip line uneven. The lip development hides the teeth, which are never fully exposed. Many male Pisceans are tall, but the females can be small and dainty. The carriage is poor, a waddling gait; the arms hug the body like fins. The overall impression is indistinct and vague. As Pisceans mature, they become heavy and are unable to control their weight.

Personality
Pisceans give a first impression of being sweet, concessive, eager to please. They are the self-effacing "gladpie"

109

of the zodiac, happy to meet everyone, to be everywhere. This kind of cloying sweetness can be tiresome. They are vacuous, and this prevents true contact. Like the fish, Pisceans are elusive and seem to slip through your fingers when you try to pin them down. They are sly, slithering, noncommittal—even when they make decisions. They are peculiar and do not seem to have any clear reason or purpose.

They do not like hard work but pursue any dream, which keeps them from getting anything done. They refuse to take a firm stand. They have a psychic power but it is seldom directed into constructive channels; in fact it seems to diminish their vitality. They rely on first impressions. They are self-indulgent and passive by nature and rarely finish what they begin.

Pisces has little control over his emotional experiences. Even when he appears undisturbed, he can be quaking within. The Pisceans' perpetual restlessness is caused by their self-imprisonment in a dreamworld away from life's responsibilities, which they are reluctant to assume. When serious facts have to be faced, Pisceans escape on aimless journeys, though they usually seek some remote and ugly place. The masochistic Pisceans like dark, secret places, for they need solitude at times and prefer to live as a hermit.

Pisceans are chronically discontented and never satisfied, for they are unable to carry out any plans to fulfillment. They try to get through with schemes and fraudulent ideas. They withdraw into a fantasy world and these fantasies can become a way of life. They are psychopathic liars and phonies but they do not often recognize the difference between what is real and what is not. The shallow Piscean lives a life of masquerade.

To make themselves appealing, to get help from others, they develop a pseudoinnocent manner that would seduce the most cynical. They smile and laugh constantly, but the laughter is empty. The face has a guileless expression but this hides a scheming mind. Pisceans do not demand like Scorpios or whine for things the way Cancerians do; they get what they want by begging for sympathy, goodwill, and ideas. They are professional panhandlers; they feed on people like leeches.

Although they seem wishy-washy, Pisceans are relentless in clinging or hanging on until they get what they need. They are tenacious but are not forceful, and one is often unaware of what they are up to. They are prideless and will affect slavish devotion, appearing to let rebuffs or insults slide off their backs. They will pander to powerful or influential people under whose aegis they can gain affluence or good standing. The female Piscean practices this ploy to perfection, and resembles the Capricorn woman in that she will do nothing for her own sex but is quite prepared to do anything for men. She is like quicksand, sucking her victims in. The Piscean man uses a gentle, self-effacing manner to get support, sympathy, and concern from a strong woman. Once he has seduced his victim, he will rob her of ideas, strength, whatever he can use, all the while maintaining the façade of innocence and helplessness.

Pisceans are swampy. They enjoy pulling their victims into their chaotic, confused lives in order to pull themselves out of the mire through the evolved minds of others.

Love
Pisceans need the constant reassurance of love. They become hurt and dejected if those around them fail to make frequent loving gestures. They get love mixed up with affection—and affection is what they really crave. Fuss over them, and their gratitude can be embarrassingly servile and effusive. Do not be too flattered when you are singled out by a Piscean, for he will cling to whoever is nearest to him. Pisceans long for love, hunger for friends, and will set about claiming you for their own. It is not necessarily you they want, however; it is the romantic atmosphere of love that sets their emotional craving into action.

When Pisceans do find someone to love, they will demand enough attention to discourage even the most patient admirer. They will pretend they are not worthy of your love to elicit reassurance, but this is playacting, an illusion they conjure up.

Piscean men choose women who have money or a social position, someone who will support them in their profession. They do not mind the domineering woman—indeed she suits them. They find security in a strong woman; demanding lovers and nagging wives give them the constant attention they need. They are the original milquetoasts. Pisces can be lied to or deceived but he will continue to go on loving an unfaithful woman; it makes her all the more precious that she is desired by other men. This is a narcissistic kind of love. Pisceans are prideless and will go through all types of humiliations to keep a lover. Pisces men are not exciting sexual partners; they are very passive, almost female in the act. Sex is not important to them, for they do not often have enough energy to perform. They dissipate what energy they have in emotional experiences. Pisceans, incidentally, are often drinkers and many become drug addicts, for this gives them a route into their fantasy world.

The female Pisceans are just as clinging as the men, even more so. Their methods are subtle, quiet, and unassuming; they will send out a smoke screen to hide the fact that they are leeches, exploiting their lovers. They need lovers or husbands who will assume full responsibility in caring for them, so that they can be free to drift through their aimless lives.

The Pisces woman does not necessarily care for a man she pursues, but she considers it a threat to her femininity if a man passes her up or eludes her attention. Piscean women must prove they are desirable. Once they win, however, they will slide back into their emotional swamp, frightened at what may be expected of them, unable to maintain their charade. One Piscean wife who had married several times finally managed to establish a firm relationship with her last husband; she would have one lover after another and spend all her emotions on them so that she could be stable and controlled with her husband. Another Pisces would have affairs with her husband's friends. When her husband died, all her lovers ran for cover and she found herself alone. When she lamented the fact that she had been deserted, that no one wanted her, a friend suggested that her unfaithfulness in marriage might have been the reason. But she couldn't understand. "That had nothing to do with it; men are just cowards." Piscean women do not see what is wrong with their own faithlessness.

One curious case I know of involved a typical Piscean girl; she had a lifeless appearance, quite washed out and ill-groomed, but she could not resist a sexual challenge. She worked in an organization that employed several homosexuals; she would go after them one at a time, sometimes managing to seduce them. Her frequent failures did not discourage her, and she did not give up the pursuit. She then discovered that one of the company's executives was bisexual, so she happily served as his procurer, sometimes even taking part herself. Naturally, her job was quite safe though she hardly ever worked at it.

Marriage

In this department Pisceans can be very practical. They want a marriage partner to be useful, to work for them. Romance is not important to them. The male is happy enough with a housekeeper who will run the home beautifully so that he can entertain his business friends. Marriage improves Pisces, makes him more decisive. With someone to support them, to cater to their cravings, Pisceans gain security and self-assurance. One Pisces husband is so happy to have a house full of children and a wife who adores him that he will often leave the office early to prepare dinner for the family.

The Pisces wife will contribute little to a marriage, since she relies on her husband for all the strength. He is the one who makes the decisions. She will drift along in an aimless way, not looking for any particular excitement or stimulation.

A marriage to a Pisces often ends strangely, with the Pisces partner simply disappearing or sliding out of the other's life. One Pisces girl married a North African and lived in Cairo with her husband; one day she decided she wanted to return to America and simply took off. After she had been in New York for several months, her husband wrote and said that he would give her three months to return or he would get a divorce and marry again. She did not even answer him, but continued to drift from one job to another. When she received notice that the divorce had gone through, she didn't say a word or even seem disturbed. She is still drifting, as far as I know.

Parenthood

The Piscean father is very emotional about his children. He fusses over them and shows them more feeling than he shows his wife. He behaves rather like a mother himself, dressing and feeding them. The children will be spoiled with too much food of the wrong sort, for Pisces is not concerned with health or intelligent diets. He eats what he feels like eating and gives his children the same. Children are his real love; there will be no discipline and he will ignore bad habits, allowing the child free rein so that the child will love him in return. As long as he is loved, the Piscean father will put up with anything his child does.

Piscean mothers also spoil their children, clinging to them and demanding affection. Often they will cripple their children with their emotional demands. One Pisces mother has a brood of illegitimate children, each one looking different from the other for they each have a different father. Her lovers come and go and she never seems disturbed to lose them, nor does a new pregnancy bother her. She just piles the kids in a car and runs off to some other town. The children are completely undisciplined and eat and sleep when they feel like it. Counseling has had no effect on her; she listens to advice with quiet contempt, then walks away silent, uncaring, determined to panhandle elsewhere for herself and her children.

Friendship

The friends of a Piscean must be prepared to give whatever is asked of them—money, help, sympathy. Pisces is clever at cultivating useful friends whose good names he can use in getting credit or a new job, or simply backing for a project. When a project falls through, Pisces will disappear just as quickly as he came and nothing will be heard from him until he needs help again. If you do not respond, Pisces will become very hurt and will complain bitterly, but he will not stick around if he is sure you see through his façade.

Career

Pisceans are lazy and will succeed at a job only if they are in complete sympathy with it and with their colleagues. They do not make good bosses, but they will work cooperatively with anyone whom they feel can be of use to them in some way. Because they deal on an emotional level, they make sympathetic listeners and can smooth over difficult situations in a firm, though they can give little real assistance. Because they understand dreamworlds and fantasy, and they love dealing with emotional entanglements, they can be successful psychiatrists. Those who believe themselves psychic will become mystics or mediums.

They are impractical and indecisive, so they do not do well in business; they become quickly bored and move on. Advertising is often attractive to them because they have a good deal of talent in creating illusion. Good-looking Pisceans will become involved with the movies or the theater; this way their fantasy lives can be given full play.

Pisces born near sunrise will have Pisces rising, and the description given will be exact.

Aries rising gives Pisces a more aggressive nature; the individual will be fair, athletic, and ready for adventure.

When Taurus rises, Pisces will be stocky, short, dark, with lovely eyes, a sweet manner, and a good complexion.

The Gemini ascendant makes Pisces shorter, thinner, more attractive and youthful, and easy to know.

Cancer, a water sign, harmonizes well with Pisces and makes a beautiful, small, soft type.

If Leo is rising, Pisces will be more important, with a fine carriage, golden coloring, and a kindly but controlled manner.

When Virgo rises, Pisces is stern, slender, positive and businesslike, with none of the usual softness.

The well-mannered Libra will give Pisces style; this is the most social Pisces. He is well-dressed and has beautiful eyes.

The powerful Scorpio ascendant will make Pisces strong and firm in attitude, heavy and handsome in appearance —a dignified combination.

The Pisces with Sagittarius rising will be tall, generous, good looking, dark, sociable, and cheerful.

The dignified Capricorn ascendant makes Pisces dark, small, and quiet, with a commanding manner.

With Aquarius rising, Pisces is usually exciting. The features are distinctive and Pisces is tall and fair, with a friendly manner.